GLADIATORS AT THE GUILDHALL

THE STORY OF LONDON'S
ROMAN AMPHITHEATRE
AND MEDIEVAL GUILDHALL

The past always looks better than it was.

It's only pleasant because it isn't here.

F P Dunne, *Mr Dooley Remembers* (1963)

Gladiators at the Guildhall

The story of London's
Roman amphitheatre
and medieval Guildhall

Nick Bateman

MUSEUM OF LONDON

Archaeology Service

First published in November 2000 by the
Museum of London Archaeology Service

A CIP catalogue record for this book is available from the British Library

ISBN 1 901992 19 5

Designed by Tracy Wellman, MoLAS

Edited by Monica Kendall

Reprographics by Andy Chopping, MoLAS

Printed in the UK by Linney Print
Mansfield, Notts NG18 4FL

**Gladiators in
combat on a sherd of
imported pottery found at the
Guildhall amphitheatre**

Contents

Acknowledgements

MoLAS gratefully acknowledges the help of the Corporation of London, who have generously sponsored all of the Guildhall site fieldwork and the continuing analysis and publication of the findings. Particular thanks are due to Ted Hartill, the City Surveyor, who oversaw the development of the Guildhall Art Gallery site – and the archaeological work which preceded it – on behalf of the Guildhall Yard East Building Committee, together with Ray Hatchard of the City Surveyors' Department and Michael Bankover, the Corporation's liaison officer for the project. More recently Gill Andrews has acted as the Corporation of London's archaeological consultant and has provided invaluable advice and support.

MoLAS's work on site was helped by many people and organisations, too numerous to mention, but special thanks are due to John Wells and Jim Crooks of WS Atkins, and Mike West of Oscar Faber, for all their patience and help over many years. Ellen Barnes of English Heritage London Division played a vital role in the implementation of the archaeological programme from the very beginning.

Within the archaeological team acknowledgement is particularly due to Gina Porter, who co-directed parts of the site with the author from 1992, and much of whose work has been made use of here. Thanks are also due to Ian Blair (site supervision), Jackie Keily (finds) and Angus Stephenson (site project management), all of whom were involved in the project for many years. Without the hard work and dedication of the whole team, comprising more than 60 MoLAS staff, none of this would have been possible. Grateful acknowledgement is also made of the contributions of Dr Richard Macphail (micromorphology – University College London) and Dr Ian Tyers (dendrochronology – University of Sheffield).

This book has benefited enormously from the comments and advice of Marietta Ryan, Gill Andrews, Dr Caroline Barron, Peter Rowsome, Jane Corcoran, Mark Samuel, Gordon Malcolm, Gustav Milne, Fiona Seeley, Angela Wardle, Geoff Egan and Damian Goodburn. Thanks are also due to Monica Kendall who has edited the final version of the text and to Peter Rowsome for post-excavation project management.

This book has been designed and typeset by Tracy Wellman. The illustrations are by Faith Pewtress (finds drawings and reconstruction drawings), Peter Hart-Allison (plans), Sarah Jones (geomatics) and Judith Dobie (reconstruction paintings). The site and studio photography is by Andy Chopping, Maggie Cox and Ed Baker. Thanks are also due to Jeremy Smith of the Guildhall Library.

A modern Ordnance Survey map with the location of the three main excavations from 1985 to 1999 shown outlined in red

Archaeologists recording a length of the arena wall on the site of the new Guildhall Art Gallery

Foreword

by the Lord Mayor

The Corporation of London and the Guildhall itself are steeped in history but when work began on the site of the new Guildhall Art Gallery in 1987 no one guessed the importance of the archaeological discoveries which would be made. The great Roman amphitheatre found buried beneath Guildhall Yard was unexpected, and the 11th-century buildings huddled in the centre of the abandoned arena are evocative of London's rejuvenation a thousand years later.

The office of Lord Mayor has existed since the 12th century and was confirmed in the Magna Carta. As the 672nd person to hold the office, it is a delight to welcome this book. It reveals that the combination of entertainment and pageantry in the annual Lord Mayor's Show and my role in promoting the City's business and international trade have an ancient echo in the gladiatorial combats of the Roman arena, attended by officials and their guests – no doubt also intent on networking throughout the known world!

London has always been a trading city, with commerce its lifeblood. These pages reveal how London's early success was often due to those who settled here – be they Celts, Romans, Saxons, Normans or Italians. Today the City of London continues to be the world's leading international financial centre. London has the vibrancy of a cosmopolitan city. This book shows that the international links we foster today have always been an integral part of the Guildhall and the work of Corporation of London.

Clive Martin

The Right Honourable The Lord Mayor
Alderman Clive Martin OBE TD DL

Preface

Every year, on the second Friday in November, the outgoing and the Lord Mayor elect come together in a chamber of the Guildhall in front of a small and select gathering of City of London dignitaries for what is known as the 'Silent Ceremony'. During the course of this ceremony, during which no words are spoken, one of the oldest symbols of the mayor's office is formally transferred between the old and new office holders. This is the so-called 'Crystal Sceptre', an ornamental mace with a crystal shaft and knob mounted in gold. The sceptre was already ancient in the Middle Ages, being reputedly of Anglo-Saxon origin, and the ceremony reinforces the City's claim to an antiquity matching that of the Crown itself.

Whatever the true origins of this fascinating object, the Corporation of London can prove a continuous line of descent as a power in England for nearly a millennium. The archaeological excavations which took place near Guildhall in 1987–99 have shown that the origins of the City are more firmly rooted in the past than even the Corporation had imagined.

The mysterious and ancient Crystal Sceptre, used in ceremonial for the inauguration of a new mayor

Beginnings

A day of discovery

It was cold, wet and very muddy in the deep hole near the City of London's Guildhall in February 1988, and the archaeological team was nearing the end of five months' excavation. Things had gone more or less according to plan. A medieval chapel had been recorded, some 17th-century burials had been found, and there were even some unexpected Roman remains – walls at unusual angles – at the bottom of the six small trenches being dug. All in all, it had been a fairly standard excavation: the archaeologists were already thinking about the next site they would work on.

One day it rained even more than usual. It wasn't possible to excavate in such weather – layers of soil turned to mud, colour distinctions could not be made out and the paper used for keeping records disintegrated. On days like this it was best to stay in the small hut used as an office, turn up the fire, and work on the backlog of complex written and drawn records.

An archaeologist trying to clean Roman timbers after heavy rain on site

A 19th-century watercolour of Roman masonry built in courses of rough stonework and red tiles set in mortar

As the excavation supervisor I was curious about the strange Roman walls: 'Why don't you draw them all on one plan', I said to one of the team, 'and check out their levels at the same time ...' Later that day we looked at the plan. The alignment of the Roman walls still looked very odd. But the strangest thing was that they all lay at precisely the same depth in the ground. And further checking revealed that they were all built in the same way – two courses of red tile at the bottom, rough stonework above, walls 1.2 metres (4ft) thick. Surely this couldn't be just coincidence? Yet how could the odd angles fit together?

I gathered the whole team, 12 of us, around the table and asked for ideas. The site archive does not record who first suggested 'What if *that* wall was curved?' but things moved fast from then. 'How many Roman buildings are there with curved walls?' ... 'It's too big for a temple' ... 'A theatre, perhaps?' ... 'No, it's an amphitheatre!'

Within a day some of the country's leading historians and archaeologists were on site. Excitement was mounting. Everyone agreed: 'You've found Londinium's amphitheatre!'

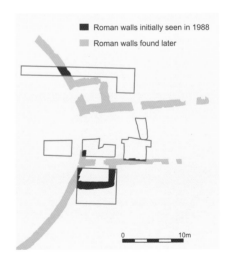

Very little of the amphitheatre was visible in the trenches excavated during 1987/88, making interpretation difficult at first

A unique opportunity

The discovery of the Guildhall amphitheatre in 1988 was proclaimed on national and international television and radio. The *Observer* (28 February) described it as 'one of the most exciting archaeological finds since the Second World War'. The *Sunday Telegraph* (6 March) called it 'one of the most important [finds] in Britain this century'. Historians and archaeologists still agree with this view.

The discovery of London's amphitheatre made national headlines in February 1988

Visiting London's amphitheatre

The stone and tile amphitheatre walls are still there today, preserved in their original location within the basement of the Corporation of London's new Art Gallery on the east side of Guildhall Yard. A long and gradual process of drying out the masonry is being undertaken before public access can be provided, but it will eventually be possible for everyone to view the remains of this fascinating monument.

In 2000 the Museum of London started work on the detailed analysis of all the records and finds, leading to the eventual publication of three volumes on the excavations at Guildhall: on the Roman, 11th-century and medieval remains. Amphitheatres are, almost by definition, exciting buildings: very few have been excavated in Britain, and London's amphitheatre had been sought, unsuccessfully, for a hundred years. The amphitheatre remains were used, much later, as the basis for a small Viking settlement. The closely packed wooden houses, animal pens, streets and an open market are among the most impressive and best-preserved 11th-century remains in Europe. Later still, in the 13th century, the site was used for the construction of London's Guildhall. This, and associated buildings such as the Guildhall Chapel, developed into the political and economic heart of the medieval City of London.

A drawing of the site under excavation in 1988. The taller walls which dominate the scene are Victorian, the amphitheatre walls lying deeper and only reached after weeks of digging

Evidently, the remains comprise much more than just a Roman amphitheatre. At every age, this site has been at the centre of the dynamic interplay between private and public in the City of London. The monuments which emerged in any period – Roman amphitheatre, medieval Guildhall – were a product of that dynamic tension: trade creating wealth; wealth demanding display; and 'public' appropriation of the 'private' monument which resulted.

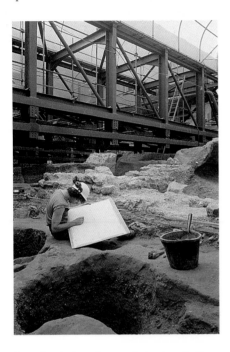

An archaeologist makes a scale drawing of a Roman wall near the east entrance to the amphitheatre

Inevitably, as the future study and analysis conducted by dozens of specialists gather pace, there will be much to add to what is contained within the following pages: some conclusions may be modified, some details will be changed. Furthermore, there is insufficient space in this book to mention all the archaeology found. But the essential, human, story is already clear; and it is so obviously one of general and immediate interest that this introduction to the site's history and archaeology has been written now, to celebrate the completion of some 13 years of fieldwork.

Public munificence

At the peak of its development in the 15th century, the Guildhall complex, with its courts, fountains, tall buildings and imposing entrances, might be described as the very model of medieval public munificence. Strangely, however, the very word 'munificence' carries distant echoes of the Guildhall's own peculiar past. The word is derived from the Latin *munus*, a gift or duty. But *munus* had another meaning as well: it was the word used by the Romans for a gladiatorial display – a show originally put on as a 'duty' by a member of the upper classes seeking preferment.

Different parts of the largest Guildhall site (1992 on) were excavated over many years as construction work progressed. The main building of the new Art Gallery contains a three-level basement where all archaeology was completely removed; in the rest of the site construction of a single basement meant that some archaeology was preserved

A simplified cross-section through the new Art Gallery and Guildhall Yard, showing the level at which the amphitheatre walls were found and are now preserved

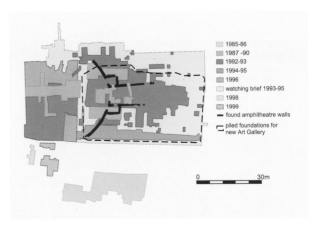

Archaeology in London

The work of MoLAS

The Museum of London Archaeology Service (MoLAS) provides archaeological services around the UK and abroad, though most of its work is concentrated within Greater London. Projects range from small test-trenches lasting a few days, to huge excavations lasting months; and from short reports for commercial clients to major books, monographs and specialist reports requiring years of research.

London is getting bigger: we read of 'pressure on the green belt'; we learn that 100 years ago places like Bexley, Chingford or Acton were in the countryside. This expansion has been going on for nearly 2000 years. But London has developed vertically as well as sideways. In the City, the heart of historic London, modern street level is up to 5 or 6 metres (almost 20ft) higher than the ground upon which the Romans founded Londinium. Ever since then Londoners have been pulling down old buildings, rebuilding, burying their daily waste, levelling the ground and starting again. London is, quite literally, built on rubbish. Peeling back those layers of rubbish, one by one, is the business of archaeology.

The archaeological team at the end of the 1993 dig

An archaeologist uncovering a human head which had been thrown into an early medieval pit

A series of plastic roofs spanning the site were used to protect the delicate archaeological remains from the weather during the 1992–3 dig

A sketch from Guildhall Yard looking east over the site in 1993. The archaeologists' site huts are stacked up on the left. A surviving Georgian building, No 1 Guildhall Yard, is on the right of the image

One could say that archaeology in London started with the workmen who uncovered a Roman kiln during Sir Christopher Wren's rebuilding of St Paul's after the Great Fire of 1666. However, it was only in the 19th century that a new hobby, 'antiquarian observation', become really popular among the middle classes. In the great Victorian rebuilding of London many chance observations – Roman mosaics, Saxon pots, medieval burials – were made, and reports sent to journals like the *Gentleman's Magazine*. After the massive destruction caused by bombing in the Second World War, huge redevelopment projects in the 1950s and 60s resulted in rescue excavations by teams of volunteers. It was soon realised that the pace of redevelopment required greater resources, and the new Museum of London's first professional archaeological unit, the Department of Urban Archaeology, was born in 1973. In 1991 this merged with other London organisations to become the Museum of London Archaeology Service (MoLAS). The Guildhall site was its first major excavation.

Antiquarian painting of Roman and medieval artefacts from the City of London

Archaeologists being filmed at work on the east end of the amphitheatre. In the foreground a metal detectorist is searching through the excavated soil for some of the thousands of metal objects recovered from the site

Archaeologists at work recording Roman walls and surfaces in the amphitheatre

A late (Red)start...

The recommencement of excavation in 1992 was held up for several weeks when a rare Black Redstart (a protected species) built its nest in bushes on the site.

Romans and gladiators

A brief history of Roman London

Britain finally entered the annals of recorded history with Julius Caesar's two 'invasions' of 55 and 54 BC. Although the Romans thought of them as barbarians, the Britons were, especially in the south-east, already very influenced by Roman culture and civilisation; and in the century following Caesar's visit there continued to be extensive trade in luxury goods, as well as political links following his treaties with the principal British tribal leaders. Roman troops may not have been stationed here but Rome certainly had friends among the Britons.

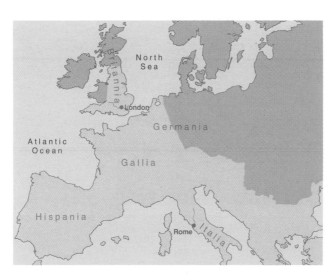

A map showing the north-western part of the Roman Empire in the mid 1st century AD

A raiding party!

The historian Strabo, writing shortly after Caesar's death, said that 'Caesar crossed twice to the island, but came back in haste, without accomplishing much or proceeding very far inland. He won two or three victories over the Britons, even though he took over only two legions, bringing back hostages, slaves and much other booty.' Britain was always seen by the Romans as very remote: writing of the behaviour of the legions in Britain during the civil wars which racked the Roman world in AD 69, Tacitus suggests that this was because 'at such a distance they were divided from the rest of the world by the Ocean'.

In AD 43 the Emperor Claudius decided to put the relationship between Rome and Britain on a more formal basis: he ordered another invasion and the complete subjugation of the island. This invasion was more thorough, with most of the south-east overrun within the first year, and the Romans, under the personal leadership of Claudius himself, seized the most important British town in the south, Camulodunum (Colchester, Essex), to turn into a military base. Campaigning then pushed towards the midlands and the west to subjugate remaining areas of resistance.

The amphitheatre, like many other public buildings in Roman London, was kept very clean, and as a result there were few objects found directly within it. These military-type fittings and brooch recovered from layers under the seating may have been lost by soldiers in the audience

Although Britain, or rather what is now England and Wales, was not fully conquered until the early 80s AD, there was clearly considerable confidence among the invaders in the early years. Some tribes in some areas were openly pro-Roman and quickly adopted Roman customs and laws. In other areas Roman settlers, usually retired soldiers, formed colonies (eg at Camulodunum).

The Emperor Claudius (reigned AD 41–54), who led the invasion of Britain. He was established as Emperor after he was found hiding behind a curtain in the palace when his nephew (the mad Caligula) was murdered. The fact that he survived for 13 years suggests he was probably not the fool Roman historians made him out to be

11

D-day landings in AD 43

Three legions landed on the south coast and worked their way quickly inland. One of the first major upsets was at the place which was later to become London (or Londinium as the Romans were to call it). The Greek historian Dio, writing over a hundred years later, describes what happened:

The Britons now fell back on the river Thames, at a point near where it enters the sea, and at high tide forms a pool. They crossed over easily because they knew where to find firm ground and easy passage. But the Romans in trying to follow them were not so successful. However the Germans [Roman auxiliary troops] again swam across, and other troops got over by a bridge a little upstream, after which they attacked the barbarians from several sides at once, and killed many of their number. But in pursuing the remainder incautiously some of the troops got into difficulties in the marshes, and a number were lost.

At some time in the late 40s AD, two small hills on the north side of the Thames (currently occupied by St Paul's Cathedral and Leadenhall Market) were selected as the site for a new town, to be run by and for the traders who handled the importing of large quantities of luxury goods (wine, oil, cloth) and the exporting of raw materials such as slaves. It was called Londinium and quickly grew to be the most vibrant town in the whole province. The town benefited from easy access to the sea, and a position at the borders rather than the centres of existing tribal groups. By the early 2nd century AD, the Roman historian Tacitus was able to describe Londinium as 'famous for its wealth of traders and commercial traffic'.

The Ermine Street Guard, a Roman re-enactment society

A panoramic view over Londinium in around AD 200 with the Thames in the background. The amphitheatre is in the lower centre, close to the rectangular fort

Miserable, misty and marginal?

Many Roman writers saw Britain as miserable, misty and marginal! On the other hand, Eumenius (secretary to the emperor Constantius Chlorus who died in York) described Britain in the 3rd century as a land that 'the state could ill afford to lose, so plentiful are its harvests, so numerous the pasturelands in which it rejoices'. Which of these views is correct?

Study of the remains of plants, animals and soils from excavations has led us to believe that widespread clearance of prehistoric wildwood – for cultivation, grazing and timber – had transformed the landscape in south-east Britain long before the Romans arrived. As a result of a worsening of the climate in the middle of the 1st millennium BC, there was a period of abandonment, but by AD 43 Celtic farmers were once again bringing parts of the London region back into cultivation.

The profiles of the original gravel and brickearth subsoils seen in excavations reveal that Londinium was founded upon two low hills, remnants of ancient floodplain terraces above the river. Similar gravel terraces follow the river up- and downstream. Ditches have been found on some of these marking Romano-British fields, probably reclaimed from the scrubby, open woodland.

By the time the Romans arrived, it is likely that only scattered trees and copses remained on much of the river's north bank, though surviving stands of oak, hazel, yew, ash and lime trees would have been carefully managed: fruit and berries collected from the woodland edge; trees coppiced to provide wattle for walls, fences and baskets; and domestic pigs left to forage in the undergrowth. In contrast, a backdrop of thick forest would still have been visible against the northern horizon, cloaking the clay soils of the higher land.

To the south lay the floodplain of the Thames, which in AD 43 was about a mile wide. Across it flowed a wide, shallow river, dividing into several channels around low sandy islands. During the 1st millennium BC the alder carr woodland on the floodplain became inundated by gradually rising river levels. By the Romano-British period it had been replaced almost everywhere by freshwater reed and sedge fen. Only the highest of the islands in Southwark, Bermondsey and Westminster remained above the encroaching tides and mudflats.

The climate improved throughout the Roman period, and by the 3rd and 4th centuries AD it was sufficiently warm and dry for olives and vines to be cultivated in Britain.

The banks of the Thames and its low sandy islands may have looked like this in the mid 1st century

British weather

Roman writers complained frequently about Britain: 'the weather tends to rain rather than snow. Mist is very common. So that for whole days at a stretch the sun is seen for three or four hours around midday' (Strabo; died c AD 23). 'A thick mist rises from the marshes, so that the atmosphere in the country is always gloomy' (Herodian; c 230s AD). 'What help to the British is the unremitting harshness, the freezing cold, of their climate?' (Claudian; c 390s AD).

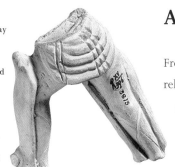

This broken clay figurine of a gladiator, found in London, shows the legs clad in greaves (body armour)

Amphitheatres and gladiators

From the first recorded examples in the 4th century BC the Games in Rome were religious in purpose and character, and were initially restricted to theatrical performances and chariot racing. Exhibitions of wild beasts as part of these games only started in the mid 2nd century BC. Chariot racing was held for the most part in Rome's Circus Maximus (the long racetrack seen in the 1959 film *Ben Hur*), and theatrical performances were given in front of the temple of the deity in whose honour the Games were held. The Games were free to all citizens – indeed they were virtually compulsory – though citizens were never permitted to participate. By the 2nd century AD the six principal sets of annual religious Games still accounted for 59 out of a total of 182 days a year for games in Rome (note that the concept of the 'weekend' had not yet been invented, though)!

Gladiator types

The word 'gladiator' comes from *gladius*, a sword. There were many types of gladiator, but the main distinctions lay in pairings of lightly and heavily armed men (speed against power; attack against defence; short weapon against long). Traditionally, spectators from the poorest farmer to the emperor himself were either *scutarii* or *parmularii* (supporters of the 'little shield' or 'big shield' gladiators). Early gladiator types included 'Gauls', 'Samnites' and 'Thracians', all traditional enemies of Rome. During the time of the emperors there was the popular pairing of *retiarius* (left-shoulder armour, net, trident and dagger) against *secutor* (short sword, oval shield, round helmet, greave on left leg). Other types included *murmillones* (heavily armed with crested helmets in the form of a fish) and *cataphracti* (with chainmail like oriental cavalry). In contrast to the recent film *Gladiator*, there is no evidence that anyone ever fought in the armour of the Roman citizen legionary. Professionals who fought with wild animals were not gladiators but *bestiarii* or *venatores*, and learnt their skills in different training schools.

A trainer overseeing the combat between a *retiarius* (left) and a *secutor* (right). Trainers were called *lanistae*, a word believed to be derived from the Etruscan for a butcher. From a mosaic at a villa in Nennig, Germany

The origins of gladiator fighting, however, are shrouded in mystery. Some scholars say that it arose in Campania in southern Italy; others that it developed among the Etruscans, in what is now Tuscany. Most people agree, however, that the tradition of making men fight for others to watch first started in the 4th century BC; and that it started as a ritual to accompany funerals. This is also what Roman writers themselves believed (like Livy, writing around the time of the birth of Christ). The first recorded 'public' showing of gladiators in Rome was in 264 BC. It was only at some time in the 1st century BC that gladiator fighting became part of the older 'official' Games.

Gladiator fights were staged in many locations: at first on open ground by the side of funeral pyres; later surrounded by special temporary stands set up in the town forum. The characteristic elliptical shape of the arena evolved to maximise viewers' lines of sight. Only much later, from the 1st century BC, did the idea of purpose-built and permanent structures come into existence. The Roman upper classes, the senators, had a real fear that permitting the construction of permanent theatres or amphitheatres, with gatherings of large numbers of citizens, could lead to public expression of political discontent – as indeed it frequently later did!.

A mosaic from Italy showing gladiators in various stages of combat. The θ (theta) sign indicates the death of the gladiator by whose side it appears (th for *thanatos*, Greek for death). Notice the gladiators' names

A gladiator's life

There is no doubt that, even for professionals, it was a risky business: most died young. At Verona, Glauco was killed in his eighth fight at 23 years old. The Syrian gladiator Flamma died at 30 after 34 fights, of which he won 21 and survived the others. In Rome, Felix died at 45 after receiving Roman citizenship from the Emperor Trajan himself. A gravestone in Orange in France commemorates another gladiator who won 53 fights. Winners and survivors frequently ended up as trainers. Gladiators might be one-off volunteers – sometimes even the hot-headed sons of senators fought for the thrill – or they might be poor citizens who sold themselves into effective slavery, signing on with a formidable oath 'I undertake to be burnt by fire, to be bound in chains, to be beaten, to die by the sword'. For the great majority, who were not, at least to some extent, voluntary recruits, 'condemned to the arena' could be *ad gladium*, meaning simple execution, unarmed, in the arena within a year; *ad bestias*, meaning thrown to the wild animals; or *ad ludos*, meaning service as a gladiator with release possible after three years – if you survived!

The earliest known amphitheatre in the Roman world (the word 'amphitheatre' comes from the Greek, meaning 'theatre on both sides') is the one at Pompeii which dates from around 80 BC. The earliest permanent theatre in Rome itself was built in 55 BC, while the earliest stone amphitheatre there was built in 29 BC by a friend of the newly proclaimed emperor Augustus. But the great explosion of building in the Empire occurred after the construction of Rome's new amphitheatre (known since the 8th century AD as the Colosseum) in the reign of the Emperor Vespasian (AD 69–79).

There was an even greater increase in the popularity of gladiator fighting between about AD 70 and AD 150. At the celebrations in Rome for Trajan's triumph over the Dacians (in modern-day Romania) at the beginning of the 2nd century, 10,000 gladiators fought, and 11,000 wild animals are reported to have been killed. The games lasted 120 days.

Details from a mosaic at Zliten, Libya, showing executions and *bestiarii*. One man is bound to a stake on wheels and pushed out to meet his death. Another man is whipped out to meet his fate. These hapless souls were probably barbarian tribesmen captured in battle. As with other mosaics it is quite possible that this records a specific show

A lead 'curse' found in the amphitheatre (above as found and below unrolled). The short inscription is probably the name of a gladiator, and the four corner holes show that it had been nailed to a wall. Similar curses have been found at other amphitheatres including Caerleon, Carthage and Trier. Many are found in underground chambers which may have been temporary mortuaries

Gladiator fighting continued until the end of the 4th century, when the official gladiator schools in Rome were closed. The last certain fights there are from the reign of Valentinian III (425–55), a time when Attila the Hun was ravaging Italy. Although the new state religion, Christianity, played a part, it does not appear to have been from concern for human rights or delicacy about the shedding of blood: the wild beast hunts, and the use of sentencing to death by wild animals, continued into the early 6th century. In the western provinces, including *Britannia*, there is no real evidence for the continuation of any of the arena traditions into the 4th century.

A still from Stanley Kubrick's 1960 film *Spartacus*

A re-enactment of gladiatorial combat was staged in front of the City's Guildhall as part of a Museum of London exhibition, drawing the crowds as well today as it must have done 2000 years previously

A day at the amphitheatre

The spectacles in amphitheatres (the original name for an amphitheatre was a *spectacula*) varied from more or less fair fights between evenly matched and well-trained gladiators, to simulated hunts in which hundreds of wild animals (many of them specially imported from North Africa) were butchered, to the mass execution and torture of 'criminals' (although the latter might include prisoners of war, slaves and, at certain periods and places, Christians). There was a convention that fighting against animals took place in the morning, proper gladiator fighting in the late afternoon, while the executions took place around midday.

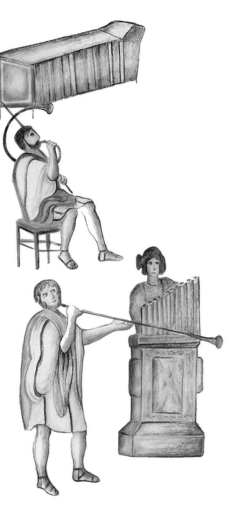

Gladiatorial shows usually began with a parade of the gladiators in full array around the arena. Who was to fight with whom was often decided by drawing lots, and the fighting was accompanied by martial music. This detail from a mosaic at Zliten in North Africa shows musicians, including a woman playing a water organ, performing in the arena

Contemporary attitudes

The Republican: The great Roman orator and lawyer Cicero writing in about 50 BC believed the arena was educational, provided only criminals suffered:

A gladiatorial show is apt to seem cruel and brutal to some eyes, and I incline to think that it is so, as now conducted. But in the days when it was criminals who crossed swords in the death struggle, there could be no better schooling against pain and death, at any rate for the eye.

The man in the street: The only surviving Roman novel, a rough and bawdy piece called the Satyricon (1st century AD), provides the perspective of the ordinary man for whom it was all just bloody entertainment:

And now we are about to have a first-class three-day show by gladiators, not a professional troop, but freedmen mostly. Titus will provide the best blades and no quarter, and a slaughterhouse in the middle so the whole amphitheatre can see … He had already procured as many toughs as you like, a woman to fight from a chariot, and Glyco's steward, who was surprised in bed with his mistress.

The emperor's adviser: With the ironic scorn of the educated classes towards the unrestrained emotions of their inferiors, Seneca (c AD 50) discusses a show in which 'criminals' were slaughtered:

I've happened to drop in upon the midday entertainment of the arena in hope of some milder diversions, a spice of comedy, a touch of relief in which men's eyes may find rest after a glut of human blood. No, no: far from it. All the previous fighting was mere softness of heart. Away with such bagatelles: now for the butchery pure and simple! The combatants have nothing to protect them: their bodies are utterly open to every blow: never a thrust but finds its mark. Most people prefer this kind of thing to all other matches … Naturally so. What good is swordsmanship? All these things only put off death a little. In the morning men are matched with lions and bears, at noon with their spectators … 'Kill! Flog! Burn! Why does he jib at cold steel? Why boggle at killing? Why die so squeamishly?'

The Christian: St Augustine of Hippo, writing in the 4th century on the subversive appeal of the arena, discusses a visit made by a Christian friend. Like Seneca he seems more appalled by the effect on the audience than the sufferings of the victims:

The whole place was seething with savage enthusiasm, but he shut the doors of his eyes and forebade his soul to go out into a scene of such evil. If only he could have blocked up his ears too. For in the course of the fight some man fell; there was a great roar from the whole mass of spectators … he was overcome by curiosity and opened his eyes, feeling perfectly prepared to treat whatever he might see with scorn and to rise above it … He saw the blood and he gulped down the savagery … drunk with the lust of blood. He was no longer the man who had come there but was one of the crowd to which he had come.

The amphitheatre: AD 70 to early 2nd century

London's amphitheatre was built, entirely in wood, in or shortly after AD 70. Many timber beams, posts and planks from this structure were found in the excavation. They were very well preserved, and accurate dates for when the trees were chopped down have been provided through dendrochronology (tree-ring-dating). Very little pottery or coins earlier than this date were found in the excavations.

Although only the eastern end of the elliptical amphitheatre was found, it is possible to calculate that it was about 100 metres by 85 metres across (ie outside to outside; the size of an average football pitch). The arena in the centre was around 60 metres across its widest. The seating area (known as the *cavea* in Latin) probably comprised between 10 and 15 tiers of wooden benches, with planks nailed to a timber framework. Entrance ways into the arena passed under the seating tiers at each end of the main axis.

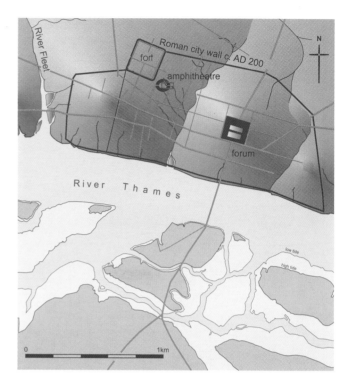

Map of Roman Londinium in about AD 200

A comparison of famous sporting arenas: the London amphitheatre superimposed on the Wembley Stadium pitch and a Wimbledon tennis court

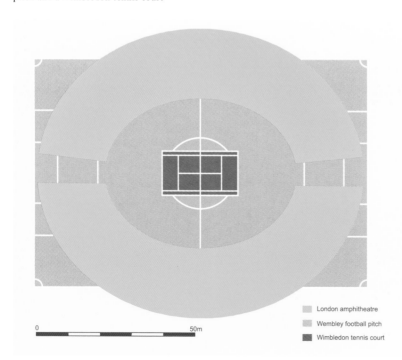

London amphitheatre
Wembley football pitch
Wimbledon tennis court

Fragments of pottery and glass showing gladiators. All found in London

20

A timber block used to support one of the posts for the amphitheatre's seating gantry. This timber had markings stamped into the surface of the wood, including the letters ICLV and MIBL. These may represent the sign of the official in charge of the supply of timber to large building projects

The oval arena had been created by digging nearly 2 metres into the natural ground and spreading out a layer of soft sand (the word *arena* means 'sand' in Latin). Around its perimeter was a timber wall, made from planks nailed to vertical squared timber posts, the bottoms of which were found in the excavation. Axe marks were still visible on these, where they had been chopped down to make way for a rebuild of the amphitheatre. Other, much larger, posts provided support for the tiers of seating around the arena, and flanked the entrance ways. Though these posts had been removed during the Roman period, the deep pits dug to house them were clearly identifiable, and in many of these there lay timber planks which had been used to support the upright posts.

A fragment of pottery from London showing a heavily armed gladiator

The arena as shown in the 1979 Monty Python film, *Life of Brian*, a black comedy!

The wooden gateway for the eastern entrance into the arena was a substantial structure, over 5 metres wide (c 16ft). Many of the lowest timbers from this were found in the dig: it was easier for the Romans to abandon than remove them. They included two very large wooden uprights, which were jointed and nailed to a long horizontal beam at ground level. The tops of the uprights had just been roughly hacked off when the amphitheatre was repaired and rebuilt. The surface of the horizontal 'threshold beam' was so well preserved that cuts and slots could easily be made out which must represent fittings for the gate's hinges and locking devices. There was also extensive wear in one small stretch suggesting that there was a smaller wicket gate to one side of the main two-leaf central gate.

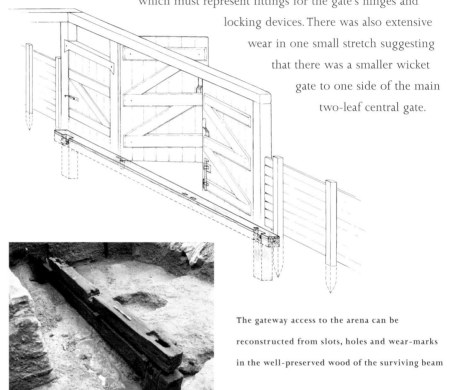

Roman timber-framing

The Romans introduced into their new province an organised timber trade, techniques such as sawing, and the concept and practice of timber-frame building: the prefabrication of solid, closely jointed frames which are then assembled on site. All of these were vital prerequisites of the ability to build elaborately shaped structures of several storeys such as the timber amphitheatre. Specific Roman introductions include tight joints such as mortice and tenon and lap-dovetails, complex scarf joints, and the widespread use of iron nails for fixing. All of these are seen at the Guildhall site, which also produced the best evidence for Roman sawyers' work in London. The techniques died out with the end of Roman rule and were not seen in England again for over 600 years.

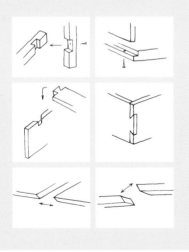

Typical Roman carpentry joints found at the Guildhall site: (clockwise from top right) nailed rebate, single dovetail corner, splayed overlap, planed mitred edges, lap dovetail, spiked half lap

The gateway access to the arena can be reconstructed from slots, holes and wear-marks in the well-preserved wood of the surviving beam

Two large timbers from the entrance way into the arena. The lower one is jointed with upright posts at each end. The gateway which existed over this threshold can be reconstructed (see above). In the 2nd century a slightly narrower gateway was erected (the higher timber, which retains the complex traces of the original structure over it)

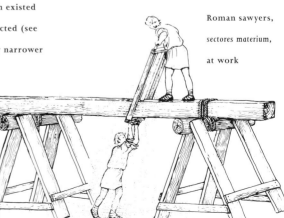

Roman sawyers, *sectores materium*, at work

The author standing in the old Roman amphitheatre at Fréjus in France, now used as a bull-fighting ring. The arrangement of large timber entrance gates and sliding timber doors for the bulls is strikingly similar to what is suggested for the London amphitheatre (see page 35)

Dendrochronology

This is the science of dating timbers from examining tree rings. Trees add a new growth ring every year, the size of which varies according to the balance of rain and sun in that year. Because every year is different, every ring is different, but the pattern is the same for all trees of the same species. Thus, by working backwards from the present day, a given pattern (like a bar code) can be matched with a particular period. If the wood is well preserved and the rings can be seen, a felling date can be worked out for most trees in the last four thousand years.

One of the large timber beams from the amphitheatre entrance way being winched off site for study and preservation

A row of deep postholes which were the settings for large timber posts flanking the entrance way into the arena (later replaced by the masonry wall to the left). Although the posts had been removed in antiquity the original timber 'chocks' on which they had been set can be seen at the base of the pits

An archaeologist sampling timbers on site (above); in the laboratory a dendrochronologist examines the sample (below)

The 'improved' amphitheatre: early 2nd to late 3rd century

The Emperor Hadrian (AD 117–38)

Hadrian was thought of as one of the 'good' emperors; for instance, he changed the law so that slaves could no longer be sold to the arena by their masters for no particular reason. He was also a connoisseur of arms, had a thorough knowledge of warfare and knew how to use gladiatorial weapons himself. Dio tells us that he travelled extensively through his empire, investigating and reforming, and 'he also constructed theatres and held games as he travelled about from city to city'. To celebrate his birthday 'he put into the arena a thousand wild beasts', while other writings tell us of a particular present he once gave: 'On his mother-in-law he bestowed especial honour by means of gladiatorial games.'

A bronze bust of the Emperor Hadrian dredged from the River Thames. Hadrian was famous for his enthusiasm for restoring or enlarging public buildings throughout the Empire

A view over the sandy arena. Isolated fragments of the arena wall can be made out curving from the bottom left to the top right of the photograph

In the early 2nd century, perhaps shortly after the visit to Britain of the new emperor Hadrian in AD 122, London's amphitheatre was given a major facelift and made larger. This involved rebuilding some of the main elements of the amphitheatre – such as the walls around the arena and those flanking the entrance ways – in Kentish ragstone and tile. Although a lot of the masonry was removed in the late Roman period, the walls survive to this day to a height of 1.5 metres (5ft) in places, and are about 1 metre thick. Double courses of red tile were used, and between three, four and five courses of roughly squared but well-laid stone. The walls were never carried higher than about 2.5 metres (8ft), being intended only to provide a facing for that part of the amphitheatre (essentially the arena area) which was dug into the ground, while the rest of the superstructure and the seating gantry were still timber. The height of the arena wall is very similar to that of other British and continental amphitheatres: essentially just enough to prevent wild animals (or angry gladiators!) leaping out of the arena and into the audience.

London's amphitheatre may have looked similar to this part masonry, part timber amphitheatre depicted on Trajan's column in Rome. The column was erected in about AD 125, to celebrate the emperor's victory in the new province of Dacia (Romania), and is decorated with hundreds of detailed scenes of soldiers and their activities

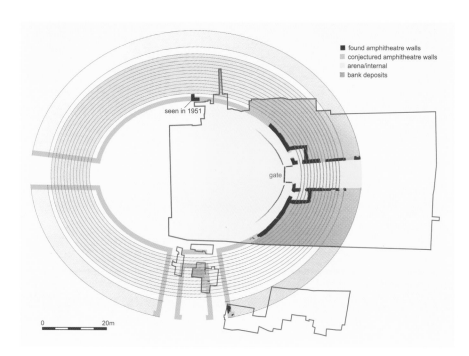

- ■ found amphitheatre walls
- ■ conjectured amphitheatre walls
- ■ arena/internal
- ■ bank deposits

seen in 1951

gate

0   20m

The remains of London's amphitheatre, found and conjectured. The small fragment of arena wall on the north side was observed in 1951 but unrecognised for what it was

Later threshold timbers of the gateway from the entrance into the arena. Set in one timber was an iron socket which had once housed the pivot of one of the gate leaves (see detail below)

We have enough of the walls to be able to make an estimate of the original size and shape of the London amphitheatre. Looking at other known amphitheatres, and using various calculations for the number of square feet per person, it could have held about 6000 spectators (to give a modern comparison, the Royal Albert Hall in London has a seating capacity of just over 5000).

The remodelled arena entrance way was about 7 metres wide (23ft), and even wider towards the exterior of the building. Timber beams had been laid at different periods of the amphitheatre's life to form thresholds for the large double-leafed gates, which opened out into the arena. Set in the upper surface of one of these timbers, which were all generally rather badly decayed, there was a rectangular iron socket, which may have acted as the pivot base for one of the gates.

An archaeologist drawing an elevation of part of the amphitheatre entrance way wall

A view looking north shows the amphitheatre as it may have appeared in around AD 120 with spectators arriving and the ceremonies to start the day's events in progress. The excavated eastern entrance with its wooden gateways is on the upper right. The amphitheatre could seat up to 6000 people – a significant portion of London's population. Dignitaries sat in the covered areas over the north and south entrances. The crowds arriving from the south and east are buying food from stalls outside the amphitheatre.

In the destruction debris around the foot of the arena wall were found two large rounded coping stones, which had fallen there during the final years of the amphitheatre's life. The remains of iron fittings were visible in the top of the curve, fixed in place with molten lead. These probably represent a railing or grillage along the top of the wall. Other slots in the stones may have been for timbers used to support the protective netting raised to stop wild animals escaping.

One of the coping stones from the arena wall which had fallen into the arena during the long decline of the amphitheatre. Holes for iron railing fixings can be seen at the top of the curve

A thick pinkish mortar had evidently been plastered on the face of the arena wall to present a smooth finish; and in a few locations scatters of brightly painted plaster were found at the foot of the wall, as if they had fallen off during the long decline of the amphitheatre, either from the wall itself or structures above it. These were of many colours, including red, black, white and blue, but no particular pattern has yet been made out. Evidence from other British amphitheatres, like Chichester, Chester and Caerleon, also suggests that arena walls were plastered and painted. At Cirencester it seems to have been done as a *trompe l'oeil*: painted to look like marble. Some of the very large amphitheatres on the Continent had scenes of combats. Analysis and reconstruction is still taking place on the London plaster.

A tile stamped with the letters PPBRLON, which stands for the Procurator of the Province of *Britannia* at London. Tiles with such stamps are commonly found near large public buildings. They may indicate official sponsorship of the amphitheatre's construction

The end of a fight in London's arena. A British slave appeals for mercy while his triumphant adversary savours his victory

An impressive range of fragments of imported marble inlays and mouldings was found in the arena, including rare and costly Egyptian and Greek porphyry. There were also a number of fragments of Purbeck marble found in the destruction deposits around the amphitheatre walls. These were quite thin and probably represent 'facings' from parts of the upper superstructure, perhaps the dignitaries' boxes (see right).

A view over the amphitheatre at the end of the excavation. The massive steel structures were required to brace the sides of the dig as excavation proceeded. Beneath the steelwork the curving wall of the arena can be made out, with the two small side-chambers flanking the entrance way

The first prepared surface in the arena was a bedding of rammed gravel mixed with hard pink mortar, over which was spread a slightly thinner layer of soft sand. The total thickness of both was about a hand's width. The combination of soft and hard layers seems to have been particularly important (it was repeated several times at the amphitheatre) and reasons for this are easy to suggest: the sand provides a soft bed to land on and to absorb impact, while the underlying harder layer prevents feet and hoofs from sinking in and gives some purchase. This very practical solution was learnt again the hard way in the mid 20th century when the makers of the film *Ben Hur* had to experiment with different surface types to stage the great chariot races round their reconstructed Circus Maximus. The elliptical arena of the London amphitheatre was large and only rarely could the management afford to resurface the whole thing: for the most part repairs were patchy as particular areas were worn away. But by the end of the amphitheatre's life ground level in the arena was over half a metre higher than its starting point.

Chariot racing in the arena: a still from the film *Ben Hur*

A small bronze figurine dressed as a Samnite gladiator, wearing a helmet with mask and holding a square shield on his left arm. His right arm may have held a sword or dagger but this is now missing

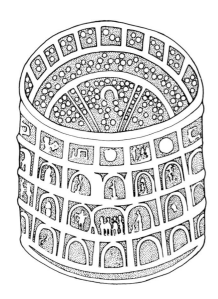

As with most of the other British examples (with the exception of Chester and Caerleon), there didn't appear to be an outer stone wall to the London amphitheatre (so it was quite different to, say, the Colosseum in Rome). The walls flanking the entrance ways became progressively less high and wide as they extended away from the arena, and the majority of deep postholes associated with the timber seating gantry were within 16 metres (c 52ft) of the arena wall (suggesting that the seating tiers did not extend back to the end of the entrance way).

The Colosseum in Rome, the largest amphitheatre in the Roman world, could seat over 50,000 people

Representation of the Flavian amphitheatre (Colosseum) on a coin minted under the Emperor Titus, son of Vespasian, in whose reign (AD 79–81) the Colosseum was formally opened. To celebrate this, Titus staged spectacular shows over 100 days with thousands of gladiators and 9000 wild beasts slaughtered. Women *bestiarii* were also exhibited

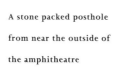

A stone packed posthole from near the outside of the amphitheatre

A possible reconstruction of the timber framework and seating around the London amphitheatre's arena

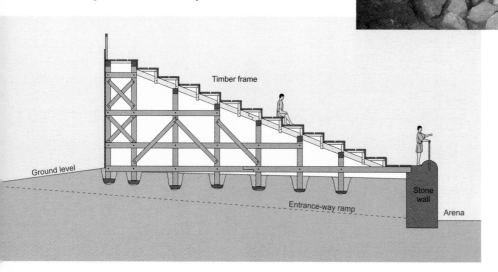

One of the support posts for the seating gantry. The planks beneath the post made it firmer and slowed down rotting from rising damp

A large timber drain ran around the perimeter of the arena. Originally it was probably covered with sand and not visible but here the timber planks which formed its lid can be seen

One of the most informative discoveries of the amphitheatre excavation was the complicated drainage system. Because the arena was, in essence, a deep hole cut into the ground, there was always going to be a potential problem with water: both rain and rising groundwater. To cope with this, the Roman architects devised a network of drains running under and around the arena and the eastern entrance. They were all housed in timber, but they ranged from simple stone-lined gullies with rough plank roofs around the perimeter of the arena to sophisticated fully carpented drains down the main axis of the amphitheatre. Not only did complex joints between timbers survive, so did the marks of the very tools used to hew them: adzes, saws, chisels and so on – in essence, a peek at a Roman carpenter's tool box.

One of the later timber drains around the perimeter of the arena can be seen on the left (viewed from above)

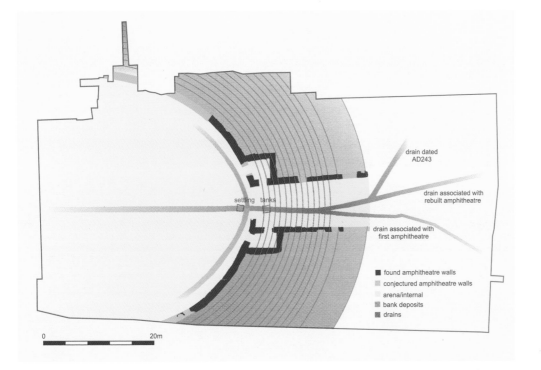

drain dated
AD243

drain associated with
rebuilt amphitheatre

drain associated with
first amphitheatre

settling tanks

- found amphitheatre walls
- conjectured amphitheatre walls
- arena/internal
- bank deposits
- drains

0   20m

The alignments of different phases of the timber drain which carried rainwater away from the amphitheatre

Bronze ligulae (surgical or cosmetic instruments) found in the early drain just outside the amphitheatre

Plumbing

Water flowing through the drains under the amphitheatre tended to carry a lot of silt and rubbish and this could have led to blocking. The Romans had very simple but effective solutions for this: the large plank-lined tank shown here lay along the course of the main drain, with water flowing in from the left side and out again, once it had filled the sump, on the right. Any silt and rubbish settled at the bottom of the sump, rather than choking the drain further down, and this could be emptied regularly in much the same way that the archaeologist is doing here – with a bucket!

Drains were rebuilt at various times throughout the lifetime of the amphitheatre. Sometimes repair was piecemeal, replacing a rotten timber here, a broken plank there; at other times a more radical overhaul was necessary. This was particularly true in the early 2nd century when the area just outside the eastern entrance of the amphitheatre seems to have turned into a boggy swamp after persistent problems with drainage in the nearby Walbrook Valley. The drains were also rebuilt at higher levels as the ground level rose in the arena. The latest timber repair of a drain for which we have specific dendrochronological-dating was in AD 243, though other dating evidence suggests that the drains and the arena surface were maintained until the very end of the 3rd century.

Oak planks expertly fitted together with 'dovetail lap-joints' as part of the amphitheatre's drain carpentry

Just three of the many Roman coins found in the amphitheatre drains

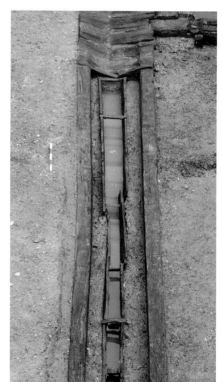

Photographs showing the central timber drain under the arena with its original timber plank roof in place (left) and then partially removed (right). The drains would originally have been covered over with sand

Southern entrance

The latest excavation on the amphitheatre was carried out in autumn 1999. Although only a small trench was dug, the excavation demonstrated conclusively that there was a southern entrance into the amphitheatre. In fact there were probably at least two entrance passages leading in from the streets to the south, perhaps joining together in a single chamber just behind the arena wall. Similar arrangements are known from several other amphitheatres in Britain and on the Continent. It is quite likely that it was through these passages under the seats that some, at least, of the audience made their way to their seats; and from them there were probably also stairs up to the *tribunalia*, the box for the presiding dignitaries, which usually lay over one or both ends of an amphitheatre's short axis.

An archaeologist records a skeleton found just behind the small fragment of amphitheatre wall in the southern entrance way to the arena. Could this have been someone killed in London's amphitheatre?

The metalled surface (see Glossary) of the ramped entrance way to the arena

A *retiarius* (net-fighter) in combat with a *secutor* (literally 'a seeker')

Animal fighting at the amphitheatre

On both sides of the amphitheatre's eastern entrance passage were two small side-chambers. Each had two doorways – one leading into the arena, one into the main entrance passage. One of the side-chambers was probably used by gladiators or fight officials as a kind of restroom, perhaps with a shrine for last-minute prayers. This was certainly the case at the Chester amphitheatre, where a similar room was excavated in the 1960s complete with its original inscribed altar stone to the goddess Nemesis (Fate), in front of which there were marks of burning on the ground where an incense brazier had stood.

A number of broken pottery sherds decorated with scenes of gladiator or animal fights were found in deposits associated with the amphitheatre. The pottery was a high-quality imported tableware. This example shows gladiators fighting bulls; beneath the bulls are the dead victims of the games

The stone altar found in a chamber at the Chester amphitheatre. The Latin inscription reads 'To the goddess Nemesis, Sextius Marcianus, the centurion, (set this up) after a vision'. Nemesis (Fate) was often equated with Diana, the goddess of hunting, and small chambers dedicated to her service have been found attached to many amphitheatres in Europe

Part of a small Roman oil lamp decorated with a boar

Part of a mosaic recording a show given in North Africa (Smirat). The show was presented by a man called Magerius, who commissioned the mosaic for his villa as testimony to his own generosity. A herald in the centre displays a tray with the bags of money spent! The show has been a simulated hunt, a *venatio*, in which expensive leopards from Africa were pitted against a band of professional touring beast fighters (*venatores*). The text records their request for payment. Diana/Nemesis, goddess of hunting and good fortune and a favourite of *venatores*, holds a large ear of wheat, a good-luck symbol

34

An archaeologist uncovers the skull of a bull left or placed in the base of the drain around the arena

A detail from a mosaic showing a *bestiarius* killing a leopard (Galleria Borghese, Rome)

While three of the chambers' door-frames were built entirely of wood (the horizontal timbers laid as thresholds were found in the excavation), one doorway, which led from the southern chamber into the arena, had two intriguing massive stone blocks as thresholds. These had clearly been reused from some earlier building, but deep narrow slots had been cut in their upper surfaces and were obviously meant to function with the entrance into the arena. Pairs of these slots, only 40 millimetres (1½ inches) apart, were set on either side of the entrance. There are no obvious parallels for them, but experts think it probable that they were part of a system for a sliding, raisable timber door. Roman amphitheatres had complex arrangements for the release of wild beasts into the arena: the most famous example is the Colosseum where a labyrinth of underground cells, passageways, movable ramps and lifts, all operated by slaves using ropes and pulleys, allowed the safe movement of hundreds of lions, tigers and other animals into the arena.

A reconstruction of the sliding timber trap at the entrance into one of the amphitheatre side-chambers. The trapdoor has been lifted and a bull has just been released into the arena

A doorway into the arena at the amphitheatre in Lepcis Magna, Libya. Vertical slots in the stones indicate a raisable trapdoor just as at London

An archaeologist cleaning the masonry of the doorway into the chamber for wild animals. The mortices cut into the threshold stones for the support beams of the sliding trapdoor can be seen on either side of the doorway

Who went to the London amphitheatre?

One of the exciting things about the timber drains was the many finds discovered in them, and the insight which these may give us on the people who visited the amphitheatre, or were associated with its functioning. The names of several hundred Roman Londoners are known from sources as varied as official inscriptions and graffiti on objects. Many of these must have visited the amphitheatre (though this can only be speculation!). At the highest level perhaps the province's governors, men such as Petillius Cerialis, a personal friend of the Emperor Vespasian; or soldiers seconded to London such as the centurion Vivius Marcianus of the Second Legion; or businessmen such as Rufus, son of Callisunus, whose name was found on a wooden writing tablet in the nearby Walbrook Valley; or a man called Turpillus who seems to have liked his drink a lot (his name was engraved on a wine jar); and perhaps even the more fortunate slaves such as Anancletus, whose work was connected with running the emperor worship cult and whose tombstone has been found in London.

Just as with football today, graffiti about individual gladiators and shows was widespread. This is from a wall in Pompeii. Much of the graffiti referred to the alleged sexual attributes of the combatants

Four pots, made locally at Highgate, were found in the rectangular drain sump

A small figurine, probably the goddess Juno, had been placed deliberately near the stone threshold of the beast chamber and was probably a votive offering

An earring, a pearl set in gold, and an enamel brooch found in the drains under the amphitheatre. Perhaps they were lost by a rich Roman woman in the audience. Contemporary writings contain many references to the attraction of rich women to well-built and successful gladiators. The eruption of Vesuvius in August AD 79 entombed the city of Pompeii, and the body of a richly dressed woman was found where she died, trying to escape from the gladiators' barracks. Women also sometimes fought as gladiators

A painting (1872) by the French artist Jean-Léon Gérôme called *Pollice Verso* (Thumbs Down). A gladiator has won his fight and awaits the signal to finish off his opponent. The right to spare a gladiator (*missio*) belonged to the person presenting the show (*editor*). But he was always influenced by the reaction of the crowd: here the Vestal Virgins in the front row express their obvious opinion (a fight announced as *sine missione* meant a fight with no possible quarter)

Decoratively carved bone hairpins are commonly found on Roman sites and would have been worn in the elaborate hairstyles that were fashionable among Roman women. These were found in the amphitheatre drains

Amphitheatres in Britain

The British contribution

Dio writes that, following his conquest of Britain, the general Plautius was 'praised by Claudius but also received an ovation. In the gladiatorial combats many persons took part, not only of the foreign freedmen but also the British captives.' Martial, celebrating the opening of the Colosseum in AD 80, describes a criminal killed by an imported Caledonian (Scottish) bear. And late Roman writings describe a show given by the Emperor Gordian in the 3rd century in which stags from Britain were hunted.

Apart from London, amphitheatre-like buildings have been identified at a number of places in Britain. All were largely earth-built structures, that is, the arena was cut into the ground and the seating bank correspondingly raised. They were comparatively simple structures, far removed from the architectural extravagance of the Colosseum and similar monumental amphitheatres. Only those at Caerleon and Chester, by the great legionary fortresses, and at the deserted town of Silchester, have been excavated to any great extent. On the other hand, several buildings which are often described in the guidebooks as 'theatres', such as at St Albans, were probably hybrid structures with at least some amphitheatre functions. Frequently this type of building is found not in a town, but linked with what might be called 'rural retreats' (pilgrimage centres with baths, temples and buildings for public shows). Examples have been found at Caistor (Norfolk), Frilford (Oxfordshire) and Gosbecks (Essex), and they were very common in Gaul (France).

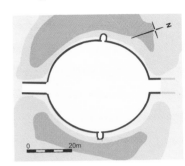

A plan of the amphitheatre at Silchester shows a masonry wall surrounding the arena and entrance ways, with steep earth banks for the timber seating behind

The amphitheatre at Caerleon in Wales was closely linked to the nearby legionary fortress and was a substantial stone-built structure. The walls, seating banks and entrance ways can all be seen. The amphitheatre was in use from the 1st century to the end of the 3rd century

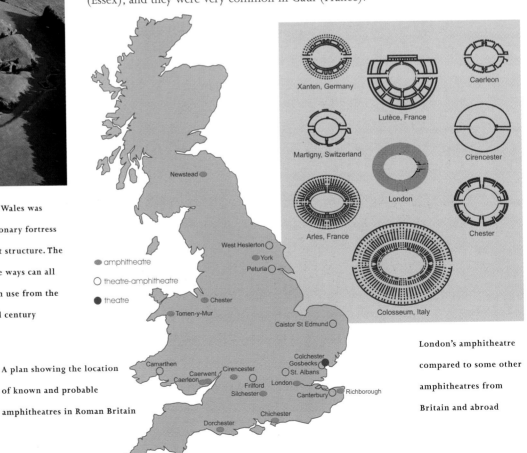

A plan showing the location of known and probable amphitheatres in Roman Britain

London's amphitheatre compared to some other amphitheatres from Britain and abroad

There is very little hard evidence for what actually went on in British arenas. There is evidence from bones found at both London and Caerleon that indigenous wild animals (boars, bears and wolves) were used, perhaps fighting each other, perhaps fighting *bestiarii*. There is some evidence for actual gladiators in the province: a gladiator's helmet found in Hawkedon, Suffolk, is very similar to types known from Pompeii; and what may be the trident of a *retiarius* was found in London. There is perhaps even archaeological evidence from St Albans that amphitheatres were used as places of public execution: a single deep post pit in the centre of the arena may have been for the stake to which criminals were tied. Though there were differences in scale, there is every reason to suspect that what went on in British amphitheatres was very similar to what went on in other Roman amphitheatres. The grim likelihood is that, over a period of more than two centuries, thousands of men and animals were slaughtered in London's arena.

A panel from a masonry frieze was found not far from the amphitheatre at Chester. It was probably from the tomb of a local *munerarius* (promoter) and shows a *retiarius* defeating another gladiator (broken off)

A 1st-century bronze helmet found near Hawkedon in Suffolk. The helmet had been 'tinned', so would have appeared bright silver, and is more than twice the weight of a legionary helmet. It is very similar to known gladiatorial helmets from Pompeii, and was indeed probably made in Italy. It has been argued that its presence in Hawkedon is a result of the sack of Roman Colchester in the Boudican rebellion of AD 60/61

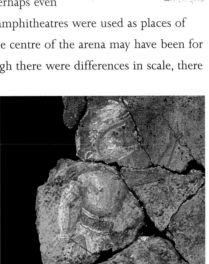

Part of a wall painting from a Roman house in Colchester. A defeated gladiator has put down his shield and holds his finger up in the standard gesture of an appeal for mercy

Gladiatorial images in Britain

There are very few British images of either gladiator or beast fighting in any form of visual decoration. One of the best known is the mosaic in the villa at Bignor, West Sussex, which shows gladiators humorously portrayed as cupids. At Brading in the Isle of Wight there is a 4th-century mosaic showing gladiators fighting. At Eccles in Kent a 1st-century mosaic also shows gladiators fighting. A mosaic in the 4th-century villa in Rudstone, Yorkshire, shows a battle between wild animals and men. A 2nd-century frieze found at Chester, not far from the amphitheatre, shows the victory of a *retiarius* over another gladiator. A 1st-century wall painting from a house in Colchester shows a defeated gladiator. Graffiti found in Leicester suggests that Lucius the gladiator loved Verecunda Ludia!

This trident head found in London may have belonged to a *retiarius* or net-fighter

Part of a mosaic found in the Roman villa at Bignor, West Sussex. A frieze shows gladiators humorously displayed as winged *erotes* (cupids). Although intentionally comic, the equipment is accurately displayed. Another panel at Bignor shows the goddess Diana, frequently linked to amphitheatres

Abandonment

The end of Roman Britain

Zosimus (a Byzantine historian writing in Greek *c* AD 500) said that in the early 5th century the British 'revolted from Roman rule and lived by themselves no longer obeying Roman laws. The Britons took up arms and, fighting for themselves, freed the cities from the barbarian pressure.' But any early successes were precarious. The Anglo-Saxon Chronicle entry for the year AD 457 tells of victory over the British natives by invading Saxons: 'in this year Hengest and Aesc fought against the Britons at a place called Crecganford and there slew 4000 men; and the Britons forsook Kent and fled to London in great terror'. (This is possibly Crayford, just south of the Thames.) Town life, organised political structures, literacy, Christianity and a money-based economy all collapsed in Britain in the 5th century.

An imagined view showing the ruins of Roman London, overgrown and crumbling in the Dark Ages

The amphitheatre was abandoned at some time in the 4th century. A layer of grey silt was found over the highest arena surface, in which were hundreds of shells of a particular type of water-loving snail. Pottery dated between AD 300–400 was also found, suggesting that it was during this period that the arena became waterlogged and silted up. Similarly dated pottery was found in deposits representing the demolition, collapse or robbing of the amphitheatre walls.

While the amphitheatre was derelict it may have been used as a municipal dump for a time. There is evidence from horse and cattle bones that whole carcasses were being dumped there, which may imply the existence of nearby butchers' shops in the late Roman period. It is also possible that the old arena was used as a slaughterhouse or market.

Domestic waste including glass, pottery and organic rubbish was thrown into the boggy ground which developed to the east of the amphitheatre

Horse, sheep and pig bones tossed into the highest fill of the latest timber drain may show how the former amphitheatre became the town dump

After abandonment most of the masonry walls were robbed, that is, the walls were dug out to make use of the building material. Most of the timber had probably already been removed before it became too rotten. Coins from the fills of the robber trenches suggest that this cannot have happened before AD 367. A lot of robbing of masonry in Roman London took place in the late 4th century to aid the repair and reconstruction of the city walls, which was a response to the widespread collapse of Roman power and authority throughout the Empire. In other areas of the amphitheatre it does not seem that the wall was robbed so much as collapsed or eroded.

After abandonment and robbing, the amphitheatre became covered over by a thick blanket of grey earth. The site of the amphitheatre lay forgotten for 1500 years, surviving only as an oval depression in the ground, a rather boggy one that was so unprepossessing that no one even tried to build over it for nearly 600 years.

The yellow sandy surfaces of the arena can be seen at the base of the image. Above them lies about 0.5m thickness of dark earth, with early 11th-century graves cut into its upper surface

Collapsed red wall plaster – the remains of a building east of the amphitheatre

A drawing showing Roman statuary and other architectural fragments reused as rubble in the core of a late 4th-century tower added to the city's defences

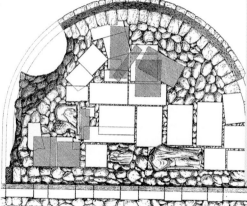

A blanket of dark earth over 1m thick lay over the abandoned remains of the Roman amphitheatre. Such deposits, which are frequently found in excavations in the City, give little clue as to what went on in the Dark Ages before London was reoccupied in the 9th century

The work of giants

The Anglo-Saxons, ancestors of the English, were in awe of Roman remains. They feared them and tried to avoid them. An Old English poem relates how 'cities are visible from afar, the cunning work of giants'. The English were much given to pondering the ravages of time: another poem notes how 'the old works of the giants stood desolate'. A poem called 'The Ruin' describes an entire town: 'wondrous is this wall-stone; broken by fate, the castles have decayed, the work of giants is crumbling'. Writing in the early 12th century, Geoffrey of Monmouth noted that 'in earlier times Britain was graced with twenty-eight cities. Some of these, in the depopulated areas, are now mouldering away, with their walls broken.' Even as late as the 14th century a monk could write of one northern town that 'it seemeth that it hath been founded by the painful labour of Romans or giants'.

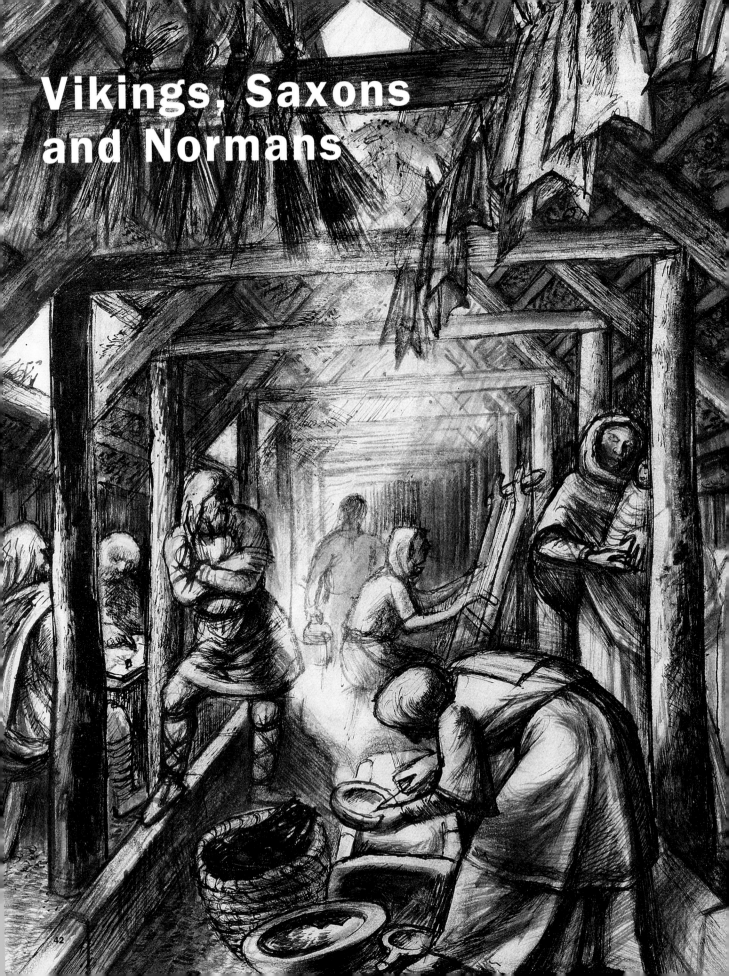

Vikings, Saxons and Normans

From St Paul's to the Normans

In AD 597 Britain re-entered the annals of European history when Augustine arrived in Kent on a mission from Rome to convert the heathen English. In AD 604 Mellitus was appointed as the first new bishop of London, though he was driven from the area after a decade and the town did not properly become Christian until AD 675. Nevertheless, by AD 640, coins were being minted again in London, the first since the collapse of Roman rule. But where precisely was 'London'?

The old deserted city within the Roman walls was reinstated as a seat of official authority, comprising the cathedral church of St Paul and possibly a royal residence. Meanwhile, outside the city walls to the west, a small settlement was established along the north bank of the river. Its earliest stages are suggested only by a few late 6th- and early 7th-century finds and burials near St Martin-in-the Fields and Covent Garden. However, in the late 7th century this early settlement developed into the major trading port of Lundenwic.

The old English word for a trading town was a 'wic'. Lundenwic is known from the writings of the 8th-century historian Bede, who described it as a 'trading centre for many nations who visit it by land and sea'. The discovery and identification of its remains outside the old Roman city, and around what is now the Aldwych ('old-wic'), has been one of the outstanding archaeological successes of the last 20 years. It was probably the largest English wic, covering some 55–60 hectares and extending from Aldwych to Trafalgar Square. Archaeology suggests that Lundenwic thrived throughout the 8th and 9th centuries.

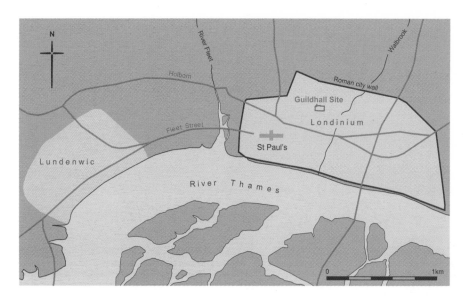

Map showing the location of Lundenwic along the Strand, and the old deserted settlement of Londinium

This reconstruction of the interior of a Viking house gives a good impression of the crowded, smoky and dark atmosphere common to timber houses of this period

At the end of the 8th century the English were themselves threatened by other barbarians. The first mention in the Anglo-Saxon Chronicle of Vikings off the coast of England is in AD 789. Later entries note that the Vikings made 'a great slaughter in London' in AD 841, and again in AD 852/3. The town was actually occupied by the Danes in AD 871 until the English king, Alfred the Great, retook it in AD 886. A decision was made then to abandon vulnerable Lundenwic and to reoccupy the old Roman city, making use of the still impressive Roman city walls: after all, London remained a frontier town, with Danish rule (the 'Danelaw') starting at the River Lea (which reaches the Thames c 6km/4 miles east of the city wall). In spite, or perhaps because, of its frontier location, the new city thrived: in the late 9th century trading quays were re-established along the Thames for the first time since Roman rule. Nearly a century of peaceful growth followed.

King Alfred

By the late 10th and early 11th centuries London was once again an internationally known trading centre; and partly as a result of its very success it became subject to renewed waves of Viking attack. Between 1013 and 1016 London was repeatedly fought over, and passed between the English under Aethelred 'the Unready', and the Danes under Swein Forkbeard and then his son Cnut. On the death of Aethelred most of the country acknowledged Cnut as king, though London and its merchants chose Aethelred's son Edmund 'Ironside'. Cnut laid siege to London unsuccessfully in 1016, but Edmund died soon after and the kingdom fell to the Danes. Cnut's reign (1016–35) and that of his sons (by different women), Harald and Harthacnut (to 1042), resulted in the brief unification of England with Denmark.

Cnut succeeded largely through his personal strengths. He went down in history as Canute the Great, the only king of England other than Alfred to achieve that honorific title. His sons, however, were less charismatic and less successful, and the northern empire assembled by Cnut soon disintegrated. His third son, Harthacnut, died childless and invited his half-brother, Edward the Confessor (Aethelred's son), to return to England from exile. He too died childless, the last of the Anglo-Saxon royal house, an event which opened the kingdom to yet another disputed succession, with rival claimants from Norway, Denmark, Normandy and England. The succession was decided, permanently, at the battle of Hastings in 1066.

Edward the Confessor

The battle of Hastings as depicted on the Bayeux Tapestry

The burial near St Paul's of a powerful Dane from around the time of Cnut (c 1035) was marked by this grave slab decorated in characteristic Scandinavian style. The runes around the edge of the slab mention two names: 'Ginne had the stone laid and Toke...'

The conquest of William the Bastard

The Anglo-Saxon Chronicle reports that, following William's arrival at the gates of London after his victory at Hastings in October 1066, Londoners 'submitted out of necessity after most damage had been done, and it was a great piece of folly that they had not done it earlier'. In spite of his annihilation of the Saxon nobility at the battle, William may not have been strong enough to take London; and besides, he needed its wealth. Negotiations may have been grudging, but the terms reached meant that life in London carried on very much as before: Londoners were probably less affected by the imposition of Norman rule than elsewhere in the country. William's declaration to the leading citizens guaranteed their property: 'I will that every child shall be his father's heir after his father's day. And I will not suffer any man to do you wrong. God preserve you.' Nevertheless, as his chaplain William of Poitiers tells us, the new king felt it advisable to surround London with strongholds like the Tower 'to contain the restlessness of its vast and savage population. For he saw that it was of first importance to hold down the Londoners.'

The arena as a cattle corral

After the amphitheatre fell out of use in the 4th century, loam and peat accumulated within the arena and over the derelict seating banks. Deposits were almost completely devoid of finds and give little clue as to their origins, but at least some of the layers were probably 'natural' (wind-blown or waterlain) in origin. Environmental evidence suggests that by the end of the 10th century all that was visible of the amphitheatre was a grassy, boggy hollow.

At some time in the early 11th century there was large-scale deliberate dumping and levelling over the whole of the arena area, filling the hollow and correcting the prevailing slopes. There is documentary and archaeological evidence for expansion and growth in the north of the thriving city at this time, and the development of such a previously abandoned area may reflect pressure for good building land. Evidence from another excavation in 1999 suggests that land immediately to the south of the former amphitheatre was occupied as early as AD 976.

Archaeologists investigate a boundary ditch, also used for drainage, with the remains of a wattle fence collapsed into it. This and other fences may have been used to corral cattle

Much of the northern part of the former arena was used for the digging of domestic waste pits throughout the 11th century. Elsewhere the remains of wattle fences and a number of deep ditches were also found, all of which probably had something to do with animal husbandry. The ditches may be attempts at water management and drainage for the boggy ground. This interpretation was borne out by the results of micromorphological analysis (see Glossary) of the nearby ground, which identified muddy areas trampled by cattle. The ditches seem to have been used both to water and, in association with the wattle fences, to corral or pen cattle. The upper fills of the ditches are dated to about 1090, after which the area was built over.

How much of the former arena was brought into use again is uncertain since its edges lay beyond the limits of the excavation. In particular, there was no material evidence for any building on the north bank of the old amphitheatre, where later in the 12th century the first Guildhall was sited. Indirect clues that there might have been a timber hall there in the 11th century are discussed below. On the east side of the old arena there is evidence, in the form of a long wattle fence, that the first houses, the cattle pens and the early church of St Lawrence were clearly fenced off from waste ground to the east.

Continuity over 1000 years: small stakes (picked out in white) from a long fence marked the east side of the Danish properties. This boundary survived to influence all subsequent buildings. Above it lie the foundations of the former Art Gallery, which itself duplicated the alignments of medieval Blackwell Hall. The concrete foundations of the new Gallery (on the right) perpetuate the same alignment

The burial ground of St Lawrence

The south-west corner of the former arena was enclosed and used as a burial ground in the early 11th century. The earliest phase of the graveyard comprised 18 burials, two of which have so far provided dendrochronology dates from the wooden boards used in the 'coffins': one of 1046 and one of 1066. One of the 'coffins' in a second phase has produced a timber date of 1086. The graves were set about 1 metre apart, and were generally rather shallow, some being no more than half a metre deep. They were carefully spaced apart from each other, in contrast with the later medieval period where intercutting was common. Around the graveyard there was a hedge or fence in which there was at least one elder tree which had been regularly coppiced during its life.

The cut-down stump of an alder tree which once formed part of a hedge beside the 11th-century graveyard

Most of the burials were contained in structures that would be better termed 'boxes' than coffins. The cleft oak or beech boards were very well preserved, and the marks of the axes used to fashion them were quite clear. The boards had been split out of huge straight old trees, probably the last of the dense 'wild-wood' which used to surround London, and were simply pegged together at the corners with slender angled dowels. The boxes did not taper to the foot in the traditional coffin shape, and often there were no head or foot boards. These simple boxes were very weak, and typical of 11th-century woodworking: they would not have withstood transportation over anything but short distances. Indeed, one of them was in fact no more than a pitched 'roof' of two boards resting against each other.

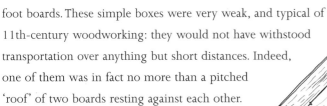

A reconstruction of an 11th-century timber coffin showing how the sides, ends and base were held together with small dowels

Excavating a burial in one of the 11th-century timber coffins found in the early churchyard of St Lawrence

Magic wands

At least five of the early 11th-century burials had hazel (or willow) twigs or 'wands' beside the body, either singly or in bunches of two or three. The wands were probably placed in the grave as symbols of Christ's resurrection, both hazel and willow being trees which, if coppiced regularly, become effectively eternal. There are parallels for this at a number of places in England during the Middle Ages, and the tradition survived as late as the early 17th century. It appears to have originated in Denmark before AD 1000 and spread from there to other parts of Scandinavia and England. One of the most important continental findspots was at Lund in south-west Sweden, a place with many other links to 11th-century London.

The burial ground was probably associated with a church or chapel – a predecessor of the later church of St Lawrence Jewry (see Glossary). No direct structural evidence for the early church was found in the excavations, but one piece of very important indirect evidence – a small fragment of rare glazed tile found in the graveyard (see right) – indicates that such a chapel may have been of very high status. It is worth noting that one of the three 'types' of church recognised by Anglo-Saxon law was the private church of a thegn (a landowner) with its own graveyard.

A burial from St Lawrence Jewry – notice the small hazel 'wands' laid over and under the body

An archaeologist cleaning a 'bier' used to transport and then lower bodies into graves. Small holes around the edges held the cords used to tie the body to the bier

A medieval manuscript showing simple early coffins

The earliest medieval building

Just by the mouth of the former eastern entrance to the amphitheatre lay a small timber building, half sunk into the contemporary ground surface. Three sides of the building were found, with walls founded on timber baseplates and with earthfast posts supporting the roof (see Glossary). There were several phases of beaten-earth flooring, and evidence of frequent repair work to the walls. Since the whole building was backfilled with dumps containing early 11th-century finds, including worked bone trial pieces with Scandinavian designs, it was almost certainly late 10th century in date. As such it is the earliest medieval activity over the whole of the abandoned amphitheatre site. Its function is unclear – although, since no hearth was identified, it is unlikely to have been a domestic house.

A sunken-floored building near the east entrance of the former amphitheatre. The floor is made of yellow clay, and holes for the large posts which supported the roof can be seen around the sides

A pig jaw bone with complicated designs of Scandinavian style carved into it, perhaps for practice. Eight such 'trial pieces' were found in the excavations; 17 similar ones have been found in an area from Cheapside to the Guildhall

London's earliest maps show very pronounced curves on the streets surrounding the amphitheatre. This plan shows the development of streets and buildings around the former amphitheatre from the 11th century

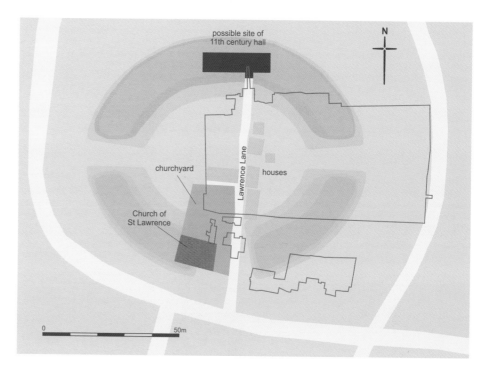

possible site of 11th century hall

N

churchyard

houses

Lawrence Lane

Church of St Lawrence

0   50m

Historic Lawrence Lane

From around the middle of the 11th century a number of domestic buildings were constructed, flanking a narrow cobbled lane which ran through and over the former arena area. It was clear that this lane remained in continuous use throughout the medieval period: at its north end there was an unbroken vertical sequence of lane surfaces up to what is now Guildhall Yard. The historic street known as Lawrence Lane – which led from the Guildhall to Cheapside past St Lawrence's Church, and parts of which can still be seen on a modern *A to Z* – is first mentioned in documentary sources in the 12th century; and it seems highly likely that this stretch of cobbling is part of the very first lane.

Excavating part of the 11th-century metallings of Lawrence Lane

The lane did not terminate with the timber buildings flanking it, but ran beyond to the north. Where was it heading towards? Archaeological evidence from other sites suggests that the area between the city wall and the Guildhall was unoccupied at this time. But does the lane represent the most persuasive evidence yet found for the existence of an early 11th-century predecessor of Guildhall? And if so, what was the function of this building?

The small excavation in autumn 1999 uncovered the southern continuation of Lawrence Lane and, most importantly, indicated that it was sited directly over the southern entrance into the former amphitheatre arena. Enough was seen in these trenches to suggest that the church of St Lawrence may have been deliberately founded on the old seating bank of the amphitheatre, possibly making use of upstanding Roman masonry. Its alignment still seems to reflect the curvature of the ancient amphitheatre. The position and shape of the Guildhall itself would also seem to have been strongly influenced by the shape of the amphitheatre seating bank. The fact that Roman masonry was seen in 1951 in the very footings of the Guildhall adds weight to the possibility that it too was built making use of the visible remains of the amphitheatre.

Leather shoe of a type common in the 10th and 11th centuries

An early 19th-century print of St Lawrence Jewry at the entrance to Guildhall Yard

Buildings in the former arena

There are clear differences between the buildings on the west and east sides of the early cobbled lane. On the west side, they were aligned 'end on' to the lane; while on the east side they were aligned parallel to it. Those on the west were exclusively wattle buildings, while those on the other side were largely built using grooved posts and planks, although they sometimes also incorporated wattlework. Micromorphology suggests that the western buildings were a classic mixture of human occupation and animal stabling, while the eastern ones seem to have been of higher status.

There was no evidence that any of the walls had ever been rendered with clay or brickearth daub, as was traditional with later medieval buildings. Instead it seems likely that turves may have been used to line the outside of wattle 'shells', to provide both insulation and extra support for the roof. This sort of construction is well known from at least the Iron Age, and survived into the late medieval period. In some of the lower-status buildings on the western side, the wattlework had been packed with dried cattle dung to the same effect.

Roofs of all the buildings were probably of some organic material such as thatch or turf, or possibly shingles (wooden roof tiles) or clapboard (overlapping horizontal boards). A number of stray shingles were found in the excavations, as well as what appeared to be three (reused) rafters.

One phase of the 11th-century buildings found over the former arena. These timber buildings were constantly being repaired, modified or extended

A reconstruction of the area of the former amphitheatre in the 11th century. A street runs over the centre of the old arena, now little more than a depression in the ground. Wattle and timber houses lie on either side of the lane. A church has been built at the south end, while a timber hall lies to the north, perhaps the forerunner of the Guildhall

Wattle-walled buildings

On the west side of the lane, the earliest and best-preserved building was rectangular, about 5 metres by 10 metres in area (c 16ft x 33ft), its walls constructed of wattlework panels set between large upright timber posts. Micromorphology suggests that mixtures of animal dung and straw were used to pack and render the wattle walls. There were no below-ground foundations, though use was made of earthfast internal roof supports and external timber buttresses or props. The building was divided into three bays, with an entrance from a cobbled alleyway to the south.

Excavating the cobbled alleyway south of the most complete wattle-walled building

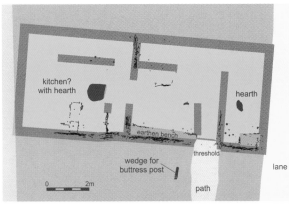

kitchen? with hearth

hearth

earthen bench

threshold

wedge for buttress post

lane

path

0   2m

Buttressed wattle and post wall construction

A reconstruction of one phase of the main wattle building on the west side of Lawrence Lane

The building was continually repaired throughout its life, often after damage by one of the frequent fires which swept through it: one of these was quite probably the London-wide fire mentioned in the annal for 1087 in the Anglo-Saxon Chronicle. Some of the repairs, such as the rebuilding of the entire south wall, were therefore fairly major. Much use was made of reused timbers, which may imply a scarcity of suitable building material.

Floors in the building were of beaten earth, and frequently required patching and repair. There was probably a centrally placed hearth, but there was also an obvious 'kitchen area' partitioned off, by a wattle wall, in the south-west corner of the building. This 'kitchen' contained several phases of plank-lined 'box hearths' set into the ground. Low 'benches', formed of turf retained by wattle, lay along the main long axis and were used for both seating and sleeping. Another wattle partition separated the eastern end of the property.

Fragments of a rare conical drinking cup fashioned from imported silver fir and found in one of the timber buildings by Lawrence Lane. The cup demonstrates a specialised trade reaching right into the heart of Europe

A miniature iron axehead. Model axeheads were popular amulets since Roman times and are known to have been used as pendants in the Viking period. However, it is unusual to find examples actually made of iron

A rare, complete, but crudely made wooden mallet was found in one of the many nearby waste pits

Excavations at another site on the north bank of the Thames in 1995 – Thames Court (near present-day Southwark Bridge) – revealed similar buildings dating from the mid 11th century; these are the only other known buildings of this type in the City of London. Although there are similarities to the well-known Viking buildings at Coppergate (York) and Dublin, there are also important differences in the position of entrances, hearths and internal roof supports. These features, and the use of angled buttress posts, suggest that a better comparison can be made with contemporary buildings at Hedeby and Lund in Scandinavia (Haithabu, near Schleswig in modern Germany; Lund in Sweden).

The cobbled pathway in front of the wattle-and-post building (the concrete columns are modern piles)

After the demolition of the wattle-and-post building, two smaller structures were erected in the same area. These were much less elaborate buildings, did not appear to have hearths and may have been used for animal stabling or some form of cottage industry. The deposition of quantities of cats' paws dumped on open ground nearby might suggest the buildings were used by a skinner.

post pits

drain

yard

0   2m

The upper end of the archaeological sequence in this area was, unfortunately, heavily truncated. But the partial remains of a quite different wattle building were found, which suggests a significant change of use. Lengths of the south and east walls survived up to a foot high (300mm), joining at a curving corner. Set on the inside of these walls were large roof-support posts set in stone-lined postholes – which indicate that the building was aisled. There was no hearth, the floors were of beaten earth, and micromorphology suggests they were covered with cattle dung. Perhaps the building was a cattle byre? A wattle-lined gully (eavesdrip) lay just outside the east wall and an open yard to the south. There seem to have been small wattle-built structures immediately to the east which may have been chicken coops.

Wattle and turf walls

The rounded wattle 'corner' of the cattle-byre building, with one stone-packed postpit in the foreground

Reconstruction of the possible cattle-byre on the west side of Lawrence Lane

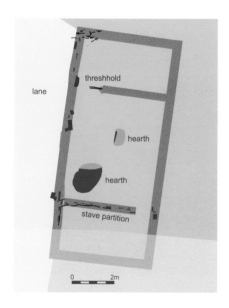

An oak seat from a home-made three-legged stool found in the earliest turf building on the east of the lane. Survival of such simple domestic furniture is very rare, and specialised furniture-making did not develop until the 13th century

The best-surviving example of the grooved posts used for the so-called *bulvaerk* building technique. Horizontal planks were slotted down the side of the grooves between two such posts 2 or 3 metres apart

A Danish-style building

On the east side of the cobbled lane (early Lawrence Lane) the buildings were different again, in both function and construction type. One of the earliest of the buildings here, probably from the mid 11th century, was a low turf-walled building, about 6 metres by 3 metres in area (c 20ft x 10ft). The seat of a three-legged stool was found inside it (it had been reused as a post support). Although small, the building had a hearth in the centre and had clearly been lived in.

The largest and most important of the buildings on the east side of the lane was built using a technique in which horizontal planks were slotted into vertical grooves carved in the sides of earthfast upright posts. There were at least seven identifiable phases of rebuilding and enlargement of this building, and evidence of repeated partial destruction by fire. A charred post from the second phase has been dated by dendrochronology to 1062, which implies that the building may have originated in the 1040s. The building appeared to have been used and maintained right through into the 12th century.

At its largest the building was about 9 metres by 5 metres (c 30ft x 16ft), and was divided into three bays (or 'rooms') by post-and-plank partitions. The hearth was centrally placed on a beaten-earth floor, and the entrance was probably at the north end of the building. There were frequent repairs, with replacing of individual posts and rebuilding of internal partitions. Micromorphology has demonstrated the cleanliness of the floors: there was very little organic debris and no trace of animal dung – a sharp contrast to the floors of the buildings on the other side of the lane. This, together with the apparently more substantial nature of these structures, indicates that they were of higher status.

A toy made from a piece of antler. It was found within the later levels (early 12th century?) of the stave building

57

Recording the brickearth floors and timber walls of the 11th-century Danish-style building

A complete post with vertical grooves had previously been found in excavations of 11th-century structures at Billingsgate, downriver from London Bridge. Its dimensions suggest a wall height of about 1.5 metres (5ft) for this kind of building, the post probably being attached by pegging to a wall plate (beam) carrying the weight of the roof. The roof of the building at Guildhall may have been shingles, as several strays were found reused as post pads or discarded as waste.

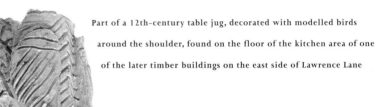

Earthfast stave and bulvaerk construction

There are very few other examples of this type of construction in London. The technique has been recorded in the lining of a well at Cheapside, in waterfront revetments dating from 1145 to 1165 at Thames Court and in the lining of a 12th-century cesspit. On the other hand, in northern Europe, and particularly in Denmark where it was still in use as late as the 18th century and known as *bulvaerk*, the technique was used extensively in early medieval buildings. Early examples include domestic houses at Hedeby and Lund.

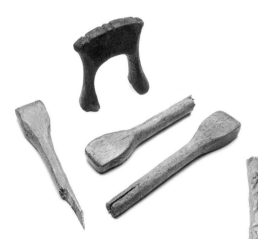

A bridge from a stringed musical instrument was found in the debris around one of the timber buildings along with three tuning pegs

Part of a 12th-century table jug, decorated with modelled birds around the shoulder, found on the floor of the kitchen area of one of the later timber buildings on the east side of Lawrence Lane

An archaeologist excavating one of the open 'cookshop' hearths

The early market area

At some time in the early 12th century the timber buildings along the eastern side of Lawrence Lane were demolished. Coincidentally this date mirrors the decline of known Scandinavian trade with London. They were replaced by unroofed temporary structures which can only be described as 'cookshops'. There were over 40 well-built hearths and ovens set in the open, with no permanent structures around or over them. These 'fast-food' outlets may have catered to people assembled in what was effectively a wide open space. We know that cooked meat was on the menu because concentrations of animal bones were found near the hearths.

Dice and gaming counter found near one of the open-air 'cookshop' hearths

Danish London in the 11th century

Though there was a Danish presence in London during the 10th century, this must have been even more marked after King Cnut's victory and accession in 1016. Cnut made London his military headquarters, with a full-time corps of trained lithsmen (warriors equally at home on land or sea, like the Vikings themselves), and there is a possibility that he maintained a 'royal palace' not far from the Guildhall excavations. There are documentary references to such a palace in the north-west of the City under the reigns of both Offa, king of the old kingdom of Mercia (757–96), and Cnut (1016–35). No direct evidence has ever been found, but the usually accepted location for this 'royal palace' is in the ward of Aldermanbury, just north-west of the Guildhall, centred on the small area around Wood Street and the east gate of the old Roman fort.

Direct evidence for Danish rule in the City has, till now, been relatively scarce. But the Guildhall excavations have produced a number of fascinating new clues on the nature of the links between England and Denmark under Cnut. Attention has already been drawn to the distinctive Scandinavian style of many of the buildings at the site, of the bone trial pieces and of the early burial practices. Individual finds from the excavations also have strong Danish or Scandinavian associations. In many of these, a name that frequently occurs by way of comparison is Lund, a town in modern Sweden which used to be part of Denmark. Significantly, Lund was only established in the 11th century, and became an important town when Cnut established a royal mint there with the help of English moneyers. It is also interesting that the cathedral church at Lund is dedicated to St Lawrence. Other indications of the significance of the Danish presence in Cnut's London can be seen in the laws, probably passed in his reign, which allowed Danish merchants to stay in the City for a whole year, a prerogative not given to other 'aliens', and to visit markets anywhere in England. When their hall was later sold to the merchants from Cologne it continued to be know as 'la saille des Deneis'. That this did not happen until the 12th century suggests that the Danish trading community remained a potent force long after Cnut's death, and was unaffected by the Norman conquest.

Lead sheeting with impression of a die for a London penny of Edward the Confessor (issue 1056–9). Possibly a trial striking, though it has been suggested that such pieces were given as receipt for payment of royal customs and dues

The palace of King Cnut

In his chronicle the monk Florence of Worcester (died 1118) wrote: 'In this year [1017] King Cnut received the dominion of the whole of England ... and at the Lord's Nativity, when he was in London, he gave orders for the perfidious ealdorman Edric to be killed in the palace, because he feared to be at some time deceived by his treachery ... and he ordered his body to be thrown over the wall of the city and left unburied.'

An image of King Cnut and his mistress Aelgyfu of Northampton. She was never acknowledged as 'Queen', unlike his official wife, Emma of Normandy

The Empire strikes back

London's success as a trading centre in the late 10th and early 11th centuries was linked to the newly revived Holy Roman Empire under the German emperors Otto I (died 973) and his descendants. Cnut married his daughter Gunnhild to the future emperor Henry III, though she died not long afterwards. Subjects of the German Empire were granted special privileges in the London markets:

and subjects of the Emperor who came in their ships were entitled to the same privileges as ourselves; besides wool which has been unloaded and melted fat they were also permitted to buy three live pigs for their ships. But they were not allowed any right of pre-emption over the burgesses, and [they had] to pay their toll and at Christmas two lengths of grey cloth and one length of brown and 10lb of pepper and five pairs of gloves and two saddle kegs of vinegar, and the same at Easter.

An 11th-century ice-skate fashioned out of bone; the hole in the toe is for a thong to tie around the foot

The reputation of the Vikings as traders was second only to their earlier reputation as warriors. Cnut's understanding of the importance of trade can be seen in his negotiations with the emperor and the pope to reduce the tolls imposed on merchants from England in Italy. In medieval London, a tribunal known as the 'Court of Husting' was held regularly in the Guildhall and dealt with matters of trade, debt, measurement and land. It was also the oldest of the assemblies and courts which constituted the organisation of the medieval City. The word 'husting' is of Danish derivation, and means an 'indoor assembly' (*hus* = house; *thing* = assembly; *Althing* is still the name of the Icelandic parliament), by contrast with the open-air 'Folkmoot' which took place just to the north of St Paul's. Whereas the latter was a gathering at which all London's male citizens were expected, the Husting was an assembly run by the town's trading elite. The Husting is first mentioned in a document of 1032 during Cnut's reign. Interestingly, its etymology implies the existence of a building (the *hus*) in which to hold such meetings at least a century before the first certain mention of the Guildhall. Could this have been the building towards which the 11th-century cobbled lane found under Guildhall Yard was leading?

Roman tiles reused as moulds to manufacture small bronze ingots. These are extremely rare in London, although they have been found in Anglo-Scandinavian contexts and have parallels in Hedeby and York

Inspecting weights and measures in an early medieval open-air market

A copper alloy hinged clasp with openwork design showing two winged animals or dragons facing each other. It was recovered from a deposit near the graveyard, along with two coins of Cnut's reign, and may have been used on a horse harness

Bones provide a subtle hint concerning the Scandinavian presence. At the Guildhall, Poultry and Thames Court excavations fragments of the skulls of four horned sheep have been found. This type of sheep is today represented in Britain by the Jacob, Manx Loughtan and Black Hebridean breeds, all of which are considered to have been derived from sheep brought to this country by the Vikings

London thrived under Danish rule. Before 1000 there were probably only a handful of churches within the city walls. Much of the rapid expansion which eventually led to the existence of over 100 parish churches by the early 12th century must have taken place in the first half of the 11th century. The late 10th and early 11th centuries were a period of dynamic expansion throughout Europe, when the power of Byzantium (the empire centred on Constantinople) was at its height. It was also a golden age for the revived Western Empire after centuries of heathen invasion and attack. The northern kingdoms in particular – English, German and Scandinavian – achieved a stability and wealth that they had never had before. Trade routes were established which would later define the whole of the High Middle Ages. Deposits in and around the timber buildings over the old amphitheatre have produced tantalising clues suggestive of these wide trading links and the high status which might be associated with such merchant activity.

A very rare lead seal from Byzantium, possibly 11th-century. The poorly registered Greek text shows that this was from the 'genikon', the office of the central financial administration in Constantinople. Found in a waste pit near the wattle buildings

This small but finely worked bronze mount for a book is probably Germanic in origin from the late 10th or early 11th century. It shows what is thought to be an Old Testament figure surrounded by vines. It may have been a decorative mount on a Bible, and was found near one of the timber buildings

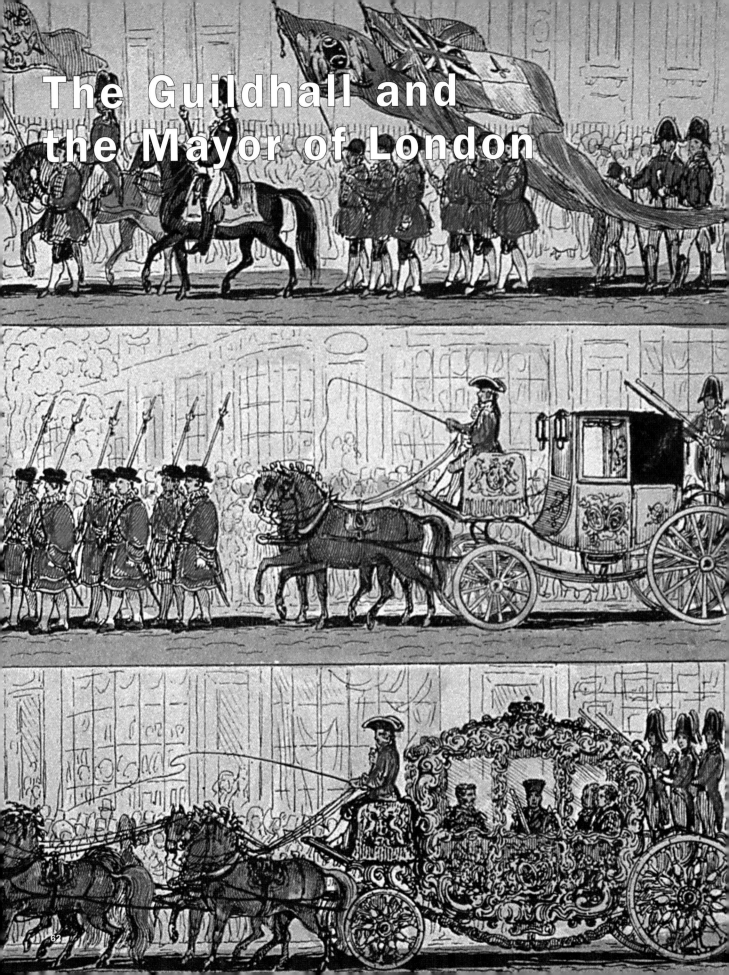

The Guildhall and
the Mayor of London

Transition: London in the 12th century

The 12th century was a time of significant change in London, and indeed Europe as a whole: the century has sometimes been labelled the First Renaissance, being a time of reawakened interest in the classical past. At a political level in England it was defined by the rise of the Plantagenet dynasty under Henry II (1154–89), one of the most powerful and able of medieval rulers. The English language appeared to have lost the battle with French: the last entries in the Anglo-Saxon Chronicle are for 1154. But in 1204, under King John, came the final separation of England from Normandy and the loss of Anjou, and this was to more or less guarantee the eventual anglicisation of the ruling classes in England. The age was marked in London by the rise of the merchant oligarchy, and the advent of London's first mayor, Henry Fitz Ailwin, in about 1189. This marked the real beginning of London's struggle for self-government under the Crown. Robert Brand, a leading citizen, cried as early as 1193: 'Come what may, Londoners shall have no king but its mayor.'

The series of fires which destroyed London in the 11th century culminated in a particularly destructive conflagration in 1136, after which many of those who could afford to do so rebuilt their houses in stone. In 1189 the first mayor issued regulations requiring party walls between buildings to be built of stone and at least 3 feet in breadth, and roofs to be tiled, in order to limit future destruction. At the end of the century sophisticated carpentry techniques were (re)introduced into England. These enabled the construction of the narrow jettied houses of three, four or five storeys which came to characterise London and other medieval cities.

London of the 11th century, with its small timber or wattle houses, few of which were more than one-storey high, would have seemed instantly familiar to the Vikings of the 10th century, or the Saxons under Alfred in the 9th. The London which emerged in the 13th century was radically different. William Fitzstephen's preface to his biography of Thomas Becket (he was a witness to his murder) describes London at the end of the 12th century: 'To this city, from every nation that is under heaven, merchants rejoice to bring their trade in ships.'

An archaeologist records the wattle lining of a 12th-century waste pit

The emergence of the City of London

Surviving documents reveal the gradual emergence of self-government in London during the 12th century. In Saxon and early Norman times order had been maintained, and revenues collected for the Crown, by the king's representatives known as 'shire reeves' or sheriffs. The division of the City into 24 (and later 26) organisational units called 'wards' is documented from at least 1127.

The origins of the wards may lie in areas of private jurisdiction of wealthy Saxon and Norman magnates, and each ward may have been required to supply a certain number of men for the defence of the town. The emergence of aldermen as leaders of the wards may have been contemporary with the creation of the Court of Husting, the assembly of London's elite. By the 13th century London was ruled by an effective oligarchy of these aldermen, and early in that century they won from the king the right to elect the mayor from among their number. The 'democratic' assembly known as the Folkmoot, for all male citizens, gradually withered away, and the land where it used to meet was built over by the early 14th century.

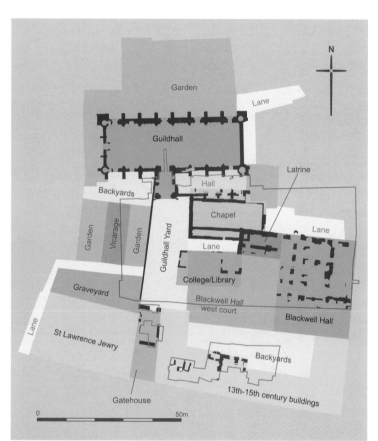

A medieval ceramic hanging lamp dating to the 11th or 12th century

The many medieval buildings excavated in part or in whole at the Guildhall excavations

A 1911 photograph showing the Lord Mayor, Aldermen and officers of the Corporation of London at the Guildhall

Saxo-Norman coins dating to the 11th and 12th centuries

An early medieval decorative stirrup mount

The Guildhall

Of all the impressive medieval buildings which once surrounded and adorned Guildhall Yard, the only one still there in any ancient form is the Guildhall itself. Although badly damaged in the war of 1939–45, as well as the Great Fire of 1666, the stone walls, towers and crypts are largely those built in the 15th century.

The first mention of what may have been the predecessor of the present Guildhall is in a document of about 1128, in which a plot of land called *terra Gialla* was leased from St Paul's at an annual rent of 2 shillings, though its precise location is unclear. In other early documents, the Guildhall or its predecessor is referred to as *Gihalle*, *Gyhale*, *Gyhhalda* and *Yeldhalle*, among other names.

There has always been debate about the precise location of the original Guildhall, but it is clear from documentary evidence that by about 1220 a building close to the current Guildhall's location was the centre of London's self-administration. In documents dating to 1232–46 it is identified as lying within the parish of St Lawrence Jewry, and deeds of the later 13th century fix the building very close to its present position. The hall was used as the centre of City government by the aldermen, and by the mayor and sheriffs who had their courts of justice there. It was also used to store London's accounts and as a secure place for its cash. Not all documents refer to such august functions, however: one shows that in 1228 and 1233 the young king Henry III used the Guildhall to store his tents.

On the left lies the Guildhall of the City of London as it is today. Most of the exterior masonry, though not the roof, dates from the 15th century. The new Art Gallery is on the right

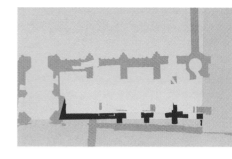

Priority: build Guildhall!

The chronicler Robert Fabyan, wealthy member of the Drapers' Company and alderman (died 1513), described the start of construction: 'In this yere also was ye Guildhall of London begon to be new edified, and an old and litell cottage made into a fair and goodly house as it now appeareth.' Nothing was permitted to get in the way of the rebuilding: City records relate that, on 2 May 1413, the mayor instructed the sheriffs that they 'should not ... allow to be taken by their officers, the two carts belonging to Henry Cook, carter; as the same were engaged upon, and belonging to, the service of the New Work at the Guildhall of London; nor were they to allow them to be in any way impeded.'

Detail from a medieval manuscript showing building labourers at work

Incorporated into the western crypt of the existing Guildhall are the fragmentary remains of a much earlier building, which architectural historians have dated to the 1280s. Excavations did not take place within or under the Guildhall itself, but evidence for a complex earlier than the existing structure was found just to the south. This included remains of a substantial masonry building with large regularly spaced buttresses projecting along one side. Most of these remains were below-ground foundations, but one pier was found with several courses of fine superstructure, including a chamfered plinth of dressed Caen stone. Remains of five similar buttresses survived to the east. The surviving plinth showed that contemporary ground level was about 3 metres (10ft) lower than now, and the architectural style suggested a 13th-century date. Documents allude to the existence of a north–south wing at the east end of the earliest Guildhall, and it may be the south end of this wing which has been identified in the excavations. This wing probably contained the hall referred to as the 'Upper Chamber' in surviving documents, where the Common Council met.

Work began on a major rebuild of the Guildhall in 1411, four years before the battle of Agincourt, under the general direction of the master mason John Croxton. It was completed in 1430, and was the largest building in the City of London after St Paul's Cathedral. This building is still standing today. The excavations added little to its history, but there was one important exception, discussed below.

Recording the internal face of a masonry wall which may be part of the early Guildhall

A close-up view of a medieval buttress, one of the few surviving superstructural elements of the 13th-century Guildhall building found on the site. The original ground level is just below the red and white scale. The two walls on either side are slightly later and hide much of the buttress

London's first historian, John Stow, dedicated his famous *Survey of London* (1598) to the Lord Mayor and citizens of London (see Glossary). Stow tells us that in 1425, during the construction of the new Guildhall, 'a stately porch entering the great Hall was erected, the front thereof towards the South being beautified with images of stone'. The internal structure and vaulting of the porch still survive, but the original ornate facade was demolished and rebuilt after a fire in 1785. Although sketches

A proposal to alter the medieval Guildhall porch rather than replace it resulted in a detailed drawn record in the late 18th century

were made shortly before its demolition, they are of limited value in trying to establish Croxton's design for what must have been the principal public face of the self-confident and powerful City. It was therefore particularly exciting to discover in the excavations 16 of the original carved stone blocks from the porch and the decorated masonry screen which adjoined its eastern side. The blocks had been reused in the foundations of the 18th-century rebuild, but were in nearly perfect condition.

Master Mason Croxton

John Croxton, master mason and architect, and disciple of Henry Yevele who built Westminster Hall, worked for the City of London for nearly 30 years. His main projects were the rebuilding of the Guildhall and its chapel, though he also worked on the rebuilding of the 'Leadenhall', the large market and storehouse off what became known as Leadenhall Street. In 1440 he asked the City for a house as a reward for his long service, and he and his wife Agnes were granted a dwelling over a new gatehouse in Basinghall Street. In 1446, after most of his work was done, he successfully petitioned the City for an increase in salary from 20 to 60 shillings per annum. He died sometime before 1451.

An architectural fragment from the medieval porch: this is part of the base of a statue niche

By combining geometrical information from the stones, with details recorded by 18th-century draughtsmen, a computerised reconstruction of the porch face is being carried out

An 18th-century watercolour showing Guildhall porch during its demolition

An architectural fragment from the medieval porch: part of a capital which once supported a statue

An architectural fragment from the late 15th-century screen connecting the porch to the chapel

The Guildhall's antiquity

The interior of Croxton's 15th-century porch has roundels at the bosses of the vaults which display the coat of arms of Edward the Confessor. It seems that even in the early 15th century the City believed, or perhaps had evidence, that the original foundation of the building went back to the 1040s.

It is now clear that Croxton's facade was more elaborate and sophisticated than the sketches made in the 18th century indicate. It was fashioned as a blind arcade with a series of canopied niches for statues of the four Virtues and various biblical figures; and several important structural elements have now been identified. Furthermore, by an amazing coincidence, four of the statues – those of Discipline, Temperance, Justice and Fortitude – were discovered in a garden in Flintshire in 1972 and have been on display in the Museum of London ever since!

Two 'Westminster' floor tiles decorated with heraldic motifs, dating from the 13th century

The Guildhall was, however, just one of a complex of buildings, set among linked courtyards and gardens, which formed the heart of the medieval City. Remains of buildings mentioned in documentary sources, as well as a few not previously known, were uncovered in the excavations and are described below.

Guildhall Chapel

Immediately south of the Guildhall, and separated from it by a narrow passage known by the 17th century as 'Cut Throat Alley', lay Guildhall Chapel. Surviving documents inform us that a chapel dedicated to St Mary, St Mary Magdalen and All Saints had been built close to the Guildhall by 1299. They describe the chapel as 'new', though it is unclear whether it replaced an earlier Guildhall chapel or how recent it was. The new chapel had an elaborate frontage and its main entrance was from the north-east corner of Guildhall Yard.

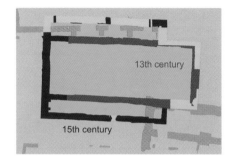

13th century

15th century

A photograph of the site taken during excavation and recording of the remains of Guildhall Chapel whose massive footings can be seen on the right

A reconstruction of the probable appearance of the Guildhall and Guildhall Chapel c 1450

Electing London's mayor

In 1406 the mayor and 'as many as possible of the wealthier and more substantial Commoners' were to meet at the Guildhall to elect a new mayor. To aid the deliberations of this august assembly the outgoing mayor ordered that a Mass should be celebrated 'in the Chapel annexed to the said Guildhall'. Following Richard Whittington's election to his second mayoralty, the commoners entreated the aldermen to make it a regular feature: 'that in future year, on the day of the Translation of St Edward [13 October], a Mass of the Holy Spirit ... should be celebrated before the election of the mayor' and that this was to be 'solemnly chaunted by the finest singers'. It was customary throughout the late medieval period to assert that the debate, and the eventual choice of the new mayor, had been guided by the Holy Spirit.

The substantial foundations of this chapel were recorded in the excavations. It had a simple rectangular nave and chancel, and archaeological evidence suggests its original frontage lay further to the west than its 15th-century replacement. Sturdy foundations of ragstone, chalk and flint were carried on arches between regularly spaced substantial piers. Five or six courses of the superstructure also survived because they were reused as foundations when the chapel was rebuilt in the 15th century and the ground level was raised. Building materials used and the architectural style confirm a late 13th-century date.

Lord Mayor Robert Titchborn, c 1656

Fragments of 'Westminster' floor tiles found near the chapel. The tiles date from the 13th century and may have been used in the chapel or Blackwell Hall

Uniforms and dress from many different centuries in the Lord Mayor's Show

Guildhall Chapel was originally associated with a semi-religious fraternity, the Society of Pui, whose members were mostly rich merchants and whose functions were largely musical and convivial. The chapel acquired a new importance for the City of London in 1406, from when it became the setting of the Mass preceding mayoral elections. Nevertheless it was not until about 1440 that construction work on the new chapel started, when John Croxton had completed the rebuilding of the Guildhall. The City had meanwhile acquired more land and, like many parish churches during the 15th century, the chapel was enlarged through the addition of aisles. Although the chapel was formally dedicated on 30 October 1444, construction work was still going on as late as 1455. Examination of the masonry styles and building materials confirmed the mid 15th-century date of the additions and modifications.

Foundation ceremonies

Two well-fashioned blocks, each about half a metre long, were found at the base of the foundations for the new aisles of Guildhall Chapel. The names Henry (Henricus) Frowyk and Thomas Knollys were painted on to the upper faces of the stones. Both of these men were notable landowners in the mid 15th century and served as mayors. In March 1440 Frowyk was appointed to serve on a committee supervising the rebuilding of Guildhall Chapel, and two years later Knollys was appointed to supervise the completion of works. The stones had clearly been laid as part of the foundation and dedication ceremony of the chapel, and represent a very rare survival. The names were intended to be 'known to God'.

A detail of the 13th-century chapel foundations with three or four courses of chequer-work superstructure above

A contemporary print showing Guildhall Chapel being demolished in the early 19th century

A plan made shortly before the demolition of the chapel in 1822 shows that there were four arches in each internal arcade, the pier bases resting on Purbeck marble slabs. Sketches made in the 18th and 19th centuries show the nave illuminated by clerestory windows, and differences in thickness of the foundations confirm that the aisles were not as high as the central nave. The ground level in the chapel hardly changed during its life, and there is no evidence to suggest that the floor level varied in different parts of the chapel – although the will of John Wells, mayor in 1431, provided for marble steps leading up to the altar.

The frontage of Guildhall Chapel as it appeared shortly before its demolition. By this date it was used as a law court

A sketch from 1822, shortly before demolition of the chapel, showing aspects of its internal appearance

A medieval latrine

The remains of a medieval public toilet! Many well-preserved finds were recovered from the cess waste which survived inside this structure

According to various medieval documents, immediately south and east of the chapel was a public latrine, though it is unclear when it was first built. This is probably the building with a 'garderobe' along one side which was found abutting one corner of the chapel (see Glossary). In fact the north wall of the latrine had been incorporated into the south wall of the 13th-century chapel, so it had clearly predated it. Furthermore, the lowest cess fills in the garderobe contained pottery dating to the early 13th century. Documents also reveal that the latrine was modified in the mid 14th century with rooms being built over it. It is unclear whether it continued in use for a while, but it was certainly demolished when the south aisle was added to the chapel in the early 15th century.

Guildhall Yard

The modern concrete slab for Guildhall Yard lay directly above a sequence of metallings and deposits which had continually raised the ground level from the 12th to the 16th century

Immediately to the south of the Guildhall, until as late as the 1970s, lay the enclosed, nearly rectangular, open space known as 'Guildhall Yard'. Documentary evidence suggests that, at least up to the middle of the 13th century, this space may have been merely the northern continuation of Lawrence Lane, then the principal means of approach from Cheapside to the Guildhall. However, by 1293 the space was deemed 'enclosed common land of the City', and from this time it is known in surviving documents as 'Guildhall Yard'. The excavations confirmed that what had been a rather narrow metalled street – with its origins in the early 11th century – was substantially enlarged and enclosed as a courtyard at some time in the mid to late 13th century. Enclosing and stretching along the whole west side of this courtyard, and still standing up to 2 metres high (almost 7ft) when excavated, was a boundary wall built of chalk and ragstone.

The hard surfaces of Guildhall Yard varied considerably in nature and extent. Some were extensive 'remetallings' over the whole Yard, others were more or less localised patchings – much as is the case with repairs to modern roads (see Glossary). Materials used ranged from rammed gravel to mixtures of chalk and stone fragments. By the time of Croxton's new Guildhall in the 15th century, ground level was some 2 metres higher than when the Yard was first established, though a proportion of this increase probably represents deliberate raising of the ground level.

Cleaning the longest surviving stretch of the early medieval wall which once flanked Guildhall Yard on its west side

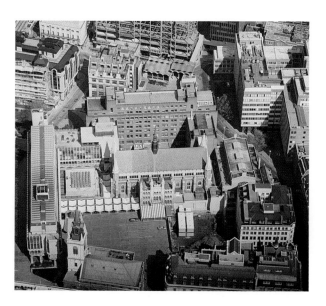

Looking down on Guildhall Yard in 1991, with the vacant plot of the 1987 excavations visible to the right of the red entrance awning

An early medieval decorated bone spoon (left); the bowl of an early medieval lead spoon decorated with a fish (above), found in the medieval surfaces of Guildhall Yard

The chantry college and library

A chantry college (see Glossary), comprising a chaplain and four priests, was established at the Guildhall Chapel in 1356. Property associated with this college, presumably including the houses where the priests lodged, is known to have lain just to the south of the chapel, and was separated from it by a narrow passage leading to the latrine described above and gardens at the rear.

A 14th-century undercroft constructed of dressed chalk blocks found in the excavation may have been a cellar for one of the college buildings. Its frontage was noticeably further to the west than the frontages of the 15th-century chapel and later Blackwell Hall, and may align with the suggested early frontage of Guildhall Chapel. Other possible foundations of the college buildings were seen in the excavations but little idea of building plans can be derived from them.

City records show that in 1425 the executors of Whittington's will built a public library for London. The exact size and site of this building are not well defined, except that it adjoined the chapel on the south side, and must therefore have made use of, or replaced, some of the earlier college buildings. According to Stow, the library building consisted of three chambers at ground-floor level, and an upper room above these in which the books were housed. The building was of stone, had a slate roof, a floor of Purbeck marble and glazed windows. Inside, the library was furnished with 28 desks to which, in the medieval fashion, the books were chained. The building was clearly imposing, with Whittington's coat of arms emblazoned in the stonework.

The old chalk undercroft, which may also have been used in the new library, was partially demolished and backfilled in the 16th century, along with other remains of the college, to make way for the expansion of Blackwell Hall.

An undercroft (cellar) built of chalk blocks, which probably formed part of the Guildhall college or library buildings

Blackwell Hall

Lying on the east side of Guildhall Yard, and sometimes described as the greatest woollen cloth market in the medieval world, the most important building connected with England's lucrative cloth trade for several centuries was Blackwell Hall. At the end of the 16th century, Stow described it as 'long since imployed as a weekly market place for all sorts of Wollen clothes broade and narrow, brought from all partes of this Realme, there to be solde'.

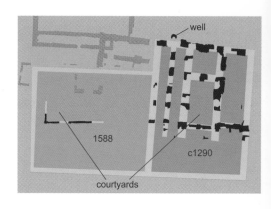

A view over two rooms of Blackwell Hall, separated by internal partition walls made of chalk blocks

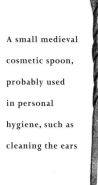

A small medieval cosmetic spoon, probably used in personal hygiene, such as cleaning the ears

An archaeologist recording a thick mortar floor used in one room of Blackwell Hall

The wool trade

From the 12th century the great centre of cloth manufacture in Europe was Flanders, fuelled by raw wool from England. The apex of this relationship was at the turn of the 14th century, by which time London was its chief port. The trade was run by the 'Company of the Staple', a guild of merchants with a licence from the king to collect customs. Because English wool had a virtual monopoly abroad, high prices were charged – allowing the merchants to make vast profits and the king to raise huge taxes. But wool was available in England at lower prices, and this encouraged the development of an English cloth industry. Between 1350 and 1450 England transformed itself into a producer and exporter of woollen cloth. The Flemish cloth industry went into decline, with many Flemish weavers migrating and setting up in England. From around 1470 English merchants controlled substantial exports of cloth through the Netherlands.

Early medieval pins,

probably used as dress fasteners

Medieval documents reveal that the origins of Blackwell Hall lie with property given by Roger de Clifford to the City of London. Great-nephew of 'Fair Rosamond', Henry II's famous mistress, Clifford played a major part in the barons' wars of the 1260s and accompanied the future Edward I on crusade. In 1293 the City gave the property to Sir John de Baukwell (or Banquelle) – from whom Blackwell Hall derives its name. In 1396 the Hall was sold by Baukwell's heirs back to the City, and Richard II granted a licence to three mercers to run it as a weekly market for woollen cloths brought from all over the kingdom. In 1397–8 the City passed legislation that made Blackwell Hall, metaphorically as well as literally, a 'closed shop'.

Black (sheep) economy

In 1397/8 it was decreed that no 'foreigner' (one not a freeman of the City) could sell, buy or show any woollen cloth in London except in Blackwell Hall. Furthermore, they were not to sell 'any manner of woollen cloth at the said Bakewellehalle, at any time in the week, exept between eleven of the clocke before Noon on Thursday, and eleven of the clocke before Noon on Saturday; on pain of forfeiture of all cloth sold to the contrary thereof'. The purported reason for this was 'the foreign drapers bringing woollen cloths to the City of London for sale, [who] sell the same in divers hostelries in secret, where they make many disorderly and deceitful bargains'. Later in the same document a much more likely reason is also given: 'and also that our said Lord the King may be better paid his customs and other duties upon the said cloths'.

An archaeologist standing in a chalk-lined well associated with Blackwell Hall

Archaeologists recording one of the internal walls of Blackwell Hall

From 1405 the Keeper of the Hall was nominated by the Drapers' Company, and the 15th century was their heyday as the controlling force of the cloth trade through London. As cloth manufactory increased in the provincial towns of England so did the number of country clothiers and drapers who wished to sell their cloth abroad. Blackwell Hall acted as the means for channelling and controlling those exports. Inside the Hall were large rooms and stalls where the cloth was pitched or stored to be sold by agents to the London merchants. These rooms were known by names such as Devonshire, Gloucester, Worcester, Kentish etc.

The coat of arms of the Drapers Company

An unused cloth seal. The central rivet would have been pressed flat when it was attached to a cloth by the authorities at Blackwell Hall. The seals certified quality and indicated that appropriate taxes had been levied on the cloth

Detail from a late 15th-century French miniature showing merchants buying and selling cloth in a covered arcaded market

Chaucer's merchant

Chaucer was the son of a London vintner. In his *Prologue* to *The Canterbury Tales* (*c* 1387), the medieval merchant was a figure of some substance, as well as a figure of fun:

There was a Merchant with a forking beard
and motley dress; high on his horse he sat.
Upon his head a Flemish beaver hat
and on his feet daintily buckled boots.
He told of his opinions and pursuits
in solemn tones, and how he never lost.
The sea should be kept free at any cost,
he thought, upon the Harwich-Holland range,
he was an expert at currency exchange.
This estimable Merchant so had set
his wits to work, none knew he was in debt,
he was so stately in negotiation,
loan, bargain and commercial obligation.

(translated by Nevill Coghill)

An early Tudor merchant from a 16th-century woodcut

Blackwell Hall's appearance

Writing from personal memory of its appearance before its rebuilding in 1588, Stow said that it was 'builded vpon vaultes of stone, which stone was brought from Cane in Normandie, the like of that of Paules church'. He refuted the legend that it had originally been a Jewish synagogue, saying that 'it had no such forme of roundnes, or other likenesse, neither had it the forme of a Church for the assembly of Christians, which are builded East and West, but contrariwise the same was builded north and south, and in the forme of a noble mans house'. Indeed he attributed its origins to a great noble family: 'for that the Armes of that family were ... so abundantly placed in sundry parts of that house ... which I my selfe haue often seene and noted before the olde building was taken downe'.

There is no surviving representation of medieval Blackwell Hall (though we do know its frontage along Basinghall Street was 112ft/34m long); nor are there documents which tell us how much rebuilding was needed for its 'conversion' from a private mansion. But the excavations have now given us much new information about this important building.

Towards the south-east corner of the site a number of rectangular pier bases were found which clearly formed part of a large medieval building: they were all built of ragstone, of more or less regular size, square to each other and with regular spacings between them. The piers formed the bases for relieving arches upon which the main walls rested. In some cases courses of these arches survived, and in even fewer some of the superstructure survived – walls about 1 metre thick. Gaps in the pattern of the foundations appeared intentional (*ie* walls and piers were definitely absent), and these probably represent the location of an internal courtyard. This appears to have been about 16 metres long and 7 metres wide (*c* 52ft x 23ft) and was aligned north–south, just as Stow described the whole building. Although in most of the site only subsurface foundations were observed, in one narrow strip stretches of the internal floors and external surfaces of the building were also seen.

Deep ragstone foundations for the walls of early medieval Blackwell Hall

A small fragment of medieval Blackwell Hall with finely dressed greensand stones forming an exterior buttress with rainwater 'flashings'. The very lowest chamfered course represents contemporary ground level. The buttress projected north from the wall forming the southern side of the central courtyard

A painted stone found in one of the post-medieval walls of the rebuilt Blackwell Hall. It probably derives from an earlier medieval version of the building. There were 27 similar stones with a variety of patterns

In the late 15th century cloth was being shipped to the Netherlands twice a year from Blackwell Hall, for sale at the great fairs of Antwerp and its neighbour Bergen-op-Zoom, by a new group called the Merchant Adventurers.

By the 1520s the General Court of the Adventurers was regulating the entire national cloth trade with the Netherlands from London. By then England was exporting every year some 80,000 finished cloths, and producing two or three times that amount for home consumption.

A Flemish painting showing the recording of civic taxes paid by local merchants (Marinus van Reymerswaele c 1540)

Merchant Adventurers

Merchants specialising in risky overseas trade ('adventurers') formed cells within existing City Companies, and from 1450 these became the nuclei of a new organisation, the Merchant Adventurers, which went on to become the principal rivals of the Clothworkers and Drapers, as well as the old declining Staple. Their business was the *shipping* of cloths; and the focus of this business was Blackwell Hall. During the great Tudor expansion of the cloth trade in the century after 1475, the economy of England was dominated by the sale of one commodity, wool cloth, and by one company, the Merchant Adventurers, exporting from London to Antwerp. Between 1550 and 1580 every Mayor of London was a Merchant Adventurer.

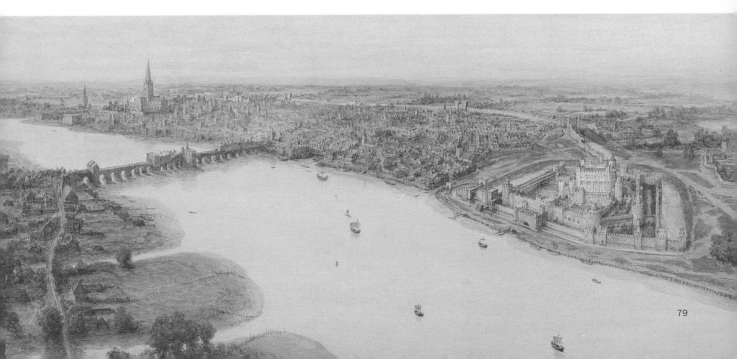

Medieval London as it might have appeared in about 1400. View looking north-west with the Tower of London in the foreground. The City was already a great trading centre

14th-century ceramic mould for buckles

St Lawrence Jewry and the Girdlers

It was probably William the Conqueror who presented the church of St Lawrence to the convent of St Savve and St Guingalaens of Montreuil in Normandy, to which it certainly belonged in the 13th century. In 1247 the church, and most of the property on the west side of Guildhall Yard, were given by the convent to a priest at St Paul's Cathedral, and by 1294 it belonged to the master and scholars of Balliol College Oxford (founded about 30 years earlier) – with whom it remained until the 19th century. By 1342 Balliol College was leasing a house and garden on the west side of Guildhall Yard to the vicar of St Lawrence for his private use.

An X-ray through an otherwise shapeless lump of corrosion clearly showing three copper alloy belt-buckles joined together

For much of its history the church of St Lawrence had links with the Girdlers, who started, like most City Companies, as a religious fraternity. The Girdlers, who made belt fittings and harness, were based in the area around Bassishaw and Coleman Street by the mid 13th century, and flourished during the 14th and 15th centuries. Girdlers' Hall in nearby Basinghall Street was certainly in use by 1439 and a modern version is still there. The church of St Lawrence was adopted as their guild church and received increasing levels of financial assistance from individual girdlers. For example, the will of the Girdlers' Master John Potyn, who died in 1333, specifically mentions moneys to be left for the burning of candles at the altar of the Holy Cross at St Lawrence Jewry.

Further evidence of associations with girdlers was found in the excavations. A complex of ovens and kilns for the manufacture of copper alloy belt-buckles was found on the west side of the Yard enclosure wall. There were at least one smelting kiln and nine melting kilns. When found, some of these kilns had ceramic moulds within them, some of which still contained buckles. Each mould could produce at least 72 individual buckles. A number of 'wasters', much copper waste or 'dross' and several hundred broken crucibles were also recovered. Clearly this was a small but productive centre for the manufacture of copper alloy belt fittings in the 13th and 14th centuries.

The only surviving part of the medieval church was a 14th-century wall and arch from the crypt beneath the 'Lady Chapel'. The medieval masonry survived when it was incorporated into a 17th-century burial vault, itself completely forgotten until its accidental discovery in 1998. The medieval church was completely destroyed by the combined effects of the Great Fire of 1666 and bombing in 1940

The gatehouse

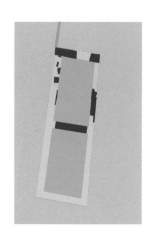

From documentary sources it is known that by 1303 the City was collecting rent for rooms at the gate of the Guildhall, and that by 1314 Guildhall Yard was closed off from Catte Street (later Gresham Street) by an inner and an outer gate. The gatehouse formed part of a range of houses along Catte Street, and by the middle of the 14th century these properties belonged to a family called Guldeford. In the 15th century the rooms above the gate were occupied by a succession of City officers.

Archaeologists recording the medieval gatehouse into Guildhall Yard

The foundations and parts of the superstructure of this well-constructed building have now been identified. The excavation revealed the northern faces of both gate piers, which were dressed with Caen stone; and the angle of the 'splay' in the masonry indicates that the gates opened northwards. The architectural style and the tool marks on the stones are typical of the mid to late 13th century. Gatehouses of this period were usually rectangular, frequently of two storeys, and often with a porter's lodge off the passageway. (A fine example survives at Kirkham Priory in North Yorkshire.) In the mid 15th century the gatehouse was rebuilt, probably for a combination of reasons, though a major factor may have been the appreciable rise in the level of Guildhall Yard after Croxton's rebuilding of the chapel and the Guildhall.

The enclosure of Guildhall Yard, and the building of a defensive gatehouse at its entrance, are all symptomatic of the struggles over consolidation of the City's powers during the 13th century. A fine gatehouse was certainly a display of status, symbolic of advances in London's economic prosperity, but it was also a necessary response to very uncertain times. Riots and rebellious behaviour were frequent in London throughout the century; particularly in the 1260s. On repeated occasions Henry III and then Edward I re-established direct royal rule of the City. They usually restored the citizens' rights to self-government, though sometimes only after long periods when the mayoralty was effectively cancelled.

The Guildhall complex at the height of its development

Football, violence and medieval London

Whatever the official face of London, its inhabitants were frequently boisterous. Even by the 15th century, Londoners' love of football (and violence) seems to have been well known. Here, a written oath has been extracted from a number of young apprentices that they should not disturb their neighbours:

Bond of John Kelsey, William Bonauntre, Ralph Spayne, Thomas Wade, Robert Hebbe, and William Bullok ... for their good behaviour ... and that none of them would in future collect money for football, or money called 'cock-silver' for a cock, hen, capon, pullet or other bird ... and that they would not thrash any ... other bird in the streets or lanes of the city, under penalty of £20.

Official proclamations from the mayor tried to encourage archery instead, 'or other semblable games which be not prohibet nor forboden by the Kynge'.

Guildhall Yard was the hub of an administrative, religious, trading and cultural enclave which reached its zenith in terms of architectural elaboration during the 15th century. With fine tall stone buildings ranged around a private courtyard entered through a gatehouse, and with other courts and gardens beyond, the complex bore more than a passing resemblance to a monastery or cathedral precinct. Other contemporary improvements or additions, which lay outside the area of archaeological investigation, included the new Mayors' Court – built to the north of the Guildhall in 1424/5 – and the 'two dismal prisons known as "Little ease"', which lay under the Hall Keepers' Office and were used to punish miscreant apprentices. One of the very last improvements came in 1501, nearly a hundred years after the start of Croxton's work: an area to the north of the Guildhall, previously occupied by gardens, was used to build new kitchens which catered for the first Lord Mayor's banquet held at the Guildhall for Sir John Shaa in 1502.

A detail from one of the earliest maps of London, made in 1559/61 very shortly after the apex of the development of the Guildhall complex, and before the effects of the Reformation. The Guildhall is in the centre

The provision of ceremony and feasts at the Guildhall is yet another sign, if one were needed, of the power and confidence of the City in the 15th and early 16th centuries. London itself was a wealthy town, and the Guildhall was its public face. It was also, just as now, a cosmopolitan town, its wealth and trade attracting many foreigners. In the 15th century a substantial proportion (about 5 per cent) of the population were 'aliens': mostly Flemings, Germans and Italians. There was, at times, an anti-alien culture in London. An Italian visiting in 1497 said that 'Londoners have … fierce tempers and wicked dispositions … they look askance at us by day, and at night they sometimes drive us off with kicks and blows of the truncheon.' Nevertheless a chronicler described London in 1413 as 'the most noble of cities, and one which has flourished with every kind of honour more than all other cities'.

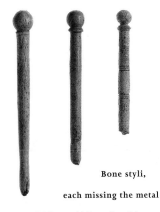

Bone styli, each missing the metal point which would have fitted into the narrow end. They were used with wax writing tablets and are frequently found on sites with scholastic or ecclesiastical associations

A lead disc found near Guildhall Chapel. It shows a deer taken as prey by a dragon, and the name (?) earl FitzRichard. This is probably a design for a personal seal, done as a trial for approval. Such seals are usually associated with officialdom and administration

Sir Christopher Clitherow,
Lord Mayor 1635

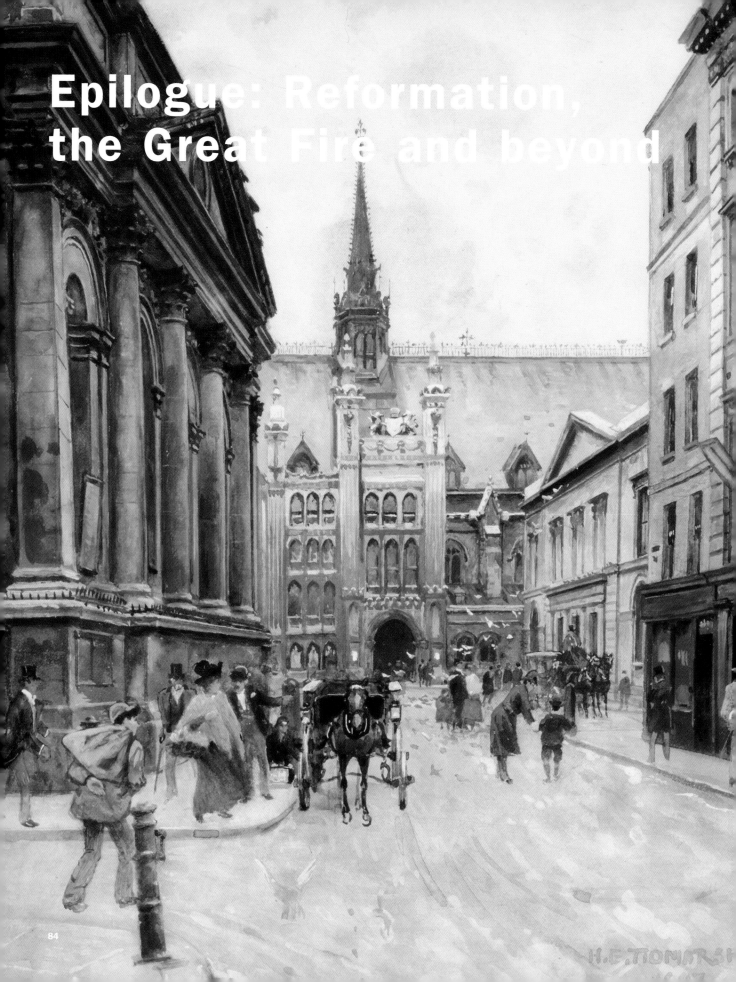

Epilogue: Reformation, the Great Fire and beyond

Destruction and change

The architectural and functional harmony of the buildings ranged around Guildhall Yard symbolised the successful fusion of civil power, religion and trade in the medieval world. This was fundamentally disrupted in the mid 16th century by the arrival in England of the Reformation. During the second half of the century the first of the buildings around the Yard was swept away in the prevailing wind of religious iconoclasm. Soon afterwards the gatehouse itself was pulled down, the Yard effectively becoming a public space.

Henry VIII was responsible for selling the possessions of England's great monasteries and abbeys. But it was his overtly Protestant son, Edward VI, and the boy-king's uncle, Edward Seymour duke of Somerset, who dissolved the religious colleges and chantries throughout the kingdom: in 1547 Guildhall College was compulsorily sold. The City managed to buy back the land, but decided anyway to pull down most of the college buildings, and to build upon the site a house 'meet for a merchant man'. This was actually occupied by the Keeper of Guildhall from the mid 17th until the late 18th century.

Whittington's library made way for the expansion of Blackwell Hall. On 6 March 1550 the City agreed that 'Sr John Aylif Knight nowe Keeper of Blackwell Hall shall have the hole lybrarye of the Guyldhall College as well above as beneth from the feste of the Anuncyacon ... so alweyes that he use and occupye the same as a common market house for the sale of clothes and none other wyse.' By the time Stow wrote this at the end of the century, the library was 'lofted through, and made a store house for clothes'.

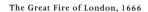

The Great Fire of London, 1666

Guildhall Yard as it appeared in about 1700

Sir John Robinson, Lord Mayor 1662

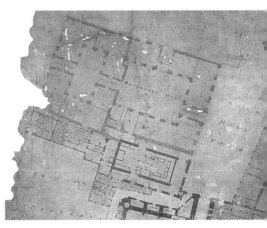

A contemporary plan of the buildings around
Guildhall Yard, c 1750

Medieval Blackwell Hall was itself subject to changes. The old Hall 'growing
ruinous and in daunger of falling, Richard May marchant Tayler at his discease
gaue towards the new building of the outward part thereof 300 pounds ...
whervpon the old Bakewel hall was taken downe, and ... the foundation of a
new strong and beautiful storehouse being laid, the worke therof was so
diligently applied, that within the space of ten moneths after to the charges of
2500 poundes, the same was finished in the year 1588'. Within 80 years this new
Hall was itself destroyed in the Great Fire.

A third version of the Hall lasted until
the final decline of the woollen cloth
market in London led to its
demolition in 1822.

The frontage of Blackwell Hall on
Guildhall Yard shortly before its
demolition in the early 19th century

The City managed to buy back Guildhall Chapel after the Dissolution, refurbishing it for its own civic use, and in this way the building survived the initial onslaught of reformist zeal. However, in April 1643, four Protestant ministers inspected the surviving medieval stained-glass windows of the chapel, concluding that images of 'pretended saints, Popes, Cardinals, monks, friars, nuns and such like ... all of which we conceive to be monuments of idolatry and superstition ... should be removed and utterly destroyed'. Unfortunately their wishes were carried out. The building survived the Great Fire, although with increasingly secular use, until it too was demolished in 1822.

Guildhall and the new law courts, c 1847

In the last great redevelopment of the area during the 1820s, the Corporation of London demolished the chapel and Blackwell Hall and replaced them with courts of law fronting on to Guildhall Yard. This was the building later converted into an art gallery and then destroyed in the Second World War. At the east end of the site, fronting on to Basinghall Street, a new building was erected for the Court of Bankruptcy. The street 'Guildhall Buildings' was also constructed at this time, with the new Mayor's Court along its south side occupying the southern half of the former Blackwell Hall site.

Of these buildings only one is still standing, No. 1 Guildhall Yard, occupied until 1992 by the Irish Society. In the 1970s the range of Georgian buildings flanking the west side of Guildhall Yard was demolished to make way for the open piazza which now exists.

The new Guildhall Art Gallery, opened in November 1999

The future

Where next?

Standing in Guildhall Yard today, visitors may perhaps find it difficult to hear echoes of the shouts, cheers and cries which once reverberated around the Roman amphitheatre. Nevertheless they may perhaps reflect for a moment on the dramatic events which have taken place here over nearly 2000 years. It is singularly fitting that the redevelopment which occasioned the excavations, and which led to the discoveries, was for a new Art Gallery. The Corporation has already preserved the walls of the amphitheatre in the basement of the new building, and is committed to allowing public access to see these remains in the future. Visitors will also notice that the outline of the amphitheatre arena has been set in stone in the design of the paving slabs of the new Yard surface.

Environmental specialist examining botanical remains

Washing some of nearly 100,000 sherds of Roman glass from the site. The remains of thousands of 1st- and 2nd-century vessels and tableware were found, the largest collection of Roman glass in Britain. They had been collected by the Romans for re-working but were never used. An early recycling scheme that went wrong!

Successful completion of the excavations means that there is now the opportunity to write the detailed history of this important public space, which has been at the centre of London civic life since the 1st century AD. The Museum of London has recently embarked upon an ambitious five-year project of research and analysis to publish this history. At the heart of the story will be a simple theme – the interplay between civic investment and private patronage – which began in the Roman period and resulted in the Guildhall Yard we see today. Our starting point will be the character and appearance of Roman Londinium's amphitheatre and its role in reinforcing and celebrating the city's place in the Roman Empire through spectacle and ritual. The redefinition of London's urban identity will then be traced from the Anglo-Scandinavian refounding of the City as a multi-cultural economic power, to its pre-eminent economic and political position in the medieval period. This changing identity, which found its final expression in the construction of the Guildhall itself, will be explored through a detailed examination of all the excavation records, finds and samples. Our aim will be to understand how past Londoners lived, worked, played and died in this corner of the City and to look at how this knowledge may change our perceptions of London's and the nation's history.

The results will be published in three Monographs: *The Roman amphitheatre*; *Anglo-Scandinavian settlement in the north-west of the City and the origins of the Guildhall*; and *The Guildhall: London's civic centre 1120–1820*. This research programme, like the excavations themselves, is being generously sponsored by the Corporation of London. The publication of the results will represent the culmination of a project which will have lasted more than 15 years, but which will encompass nearly 2000 years of the capital's history.

Glossary

Chantry Refers to the medieval Christian tradition, common between the 11th and 16th centuries, of endowing a chaplain, or a small 'college' of priests, at a church or chapel to sing ('chant') masses for the soul of the founder or his family.

Copper alloy The general term used to describe a metal whose main component is copper, but which has deliberate additions of tin, zinc and/or lead in varying proportions. Brass and bronze are well known examples.

Coppicing The regular cutting down of hazel, willow or alder undergrowth in managed woods to provide the thin branches used in basketmaking, wattle walls and many other structures. Most medieval woods were coppiced at regular intervals (frequently every seven years).

Dark Ages The confused period between roughly AD 400 and 800, for which there are few historical records, in which the existing Romano-British social system collapsed, gave way to and ultimately merged with that of the invading English peoples (Angles, Saxons and Jutes).

Garderobe The polite medieval term for a latrine or 'privy', related to the word 'wardrobe', which originally meant a chamber used to store clothes and to dress in. The garderobe was usually attached to the main rooms of a house, often at first-floor level or higher, and set into the thickness of the walls. A chute led down to a cesspit below or outside the building.

Jetty Refers to the way medieval houses projected over the streets, each storey overhanging the one beneath.

Levels Archaeologists record the height (relative to 0.00 metres, mean sea level at Newlyn in Cornwall) of each layer or feature, which helps to establish their relationship to each other in time and space.

Micromorphology The science of microscopic analysis of soil horizons, whether natural or manmade, to discover the processes behind their formation.

Road metallings Archaeologists refer to the compacted materials, such as gravel or crushed stone, used in the past to surface roads as 'metallings'.

Romans Ruled what they called *Britannia* (roughly England, Wales and parts of Scotland) from AD 43 to about AD 410, when the last Roman troops were withdrawn. The London amphitheatre was in use from AD 70 to about AD 300.

St Lawrence Jewry Lawrence was one of Rome's most famous martyrs. He was a deacon of Rome and was put to death in AD 258. A legend says he was roasted on a gridiron, but he was possibly beheaded. He was buried just outside the city walls – where the ancient church of San Lorenzo fuori le mura stands today. His execution was a major impetus for mass conversion. In England, just before the Reformation, there were over 200 churches dedicated to him. 'Jewry' means the church was in an area were Jews lived before they were expelled from England in the 13th century.

John Stow (c 1525–1605) Born in the City of London, Stow was a tailor by trade, but devoted himself to searching for antiquities, writing, and spending the little money he had on buying books, documents and manuscripts. He was known as a cheerful, indefatigable researcher who cared only for the truth. *The Survey of London* was his final work, written in his seventies. He was so poor that, just before his death, the king authorised him to set up basins for voluntary contributions in the street (but without much success). He is buried in the church of St Andrew Undershaft.

Timber construction There are many specialist terms for individual timbers in buildings. Where a building did not have masonry foundations the large upright posts might be set directly in the ground (**earthfast**), or they might sit upon horizontal timber **baseplates** or **post pads** to slow down decay. Vertical posts were jointed at the top to another horizontal beam, the **wall plate,** upon which the roof **rafters** rested.

Vikings A mixture of raiders from Scandinavia (Danes and Norsemen) who harried the coasts of Europe in an explosion of violence from the 9th to the 11th centuries. By the time they finally conquered England in 1016 they were Christian and hardly to be distinguished from the English.

Wattlework The interweaving of slender branches over each other and around slightly thicker branches at right angles to them. Wattlework was used for small objects like baskets, and large panels in walls or fences. **Daub** was applied as a wet slurry of mud or dung to the wattle, where it dried out to become more or less weatherproof, giving the wall strength and depth.

Further reading

J P V D Balsdon, *Life and leisure in Ancient Rome*, 1969

Caroline Barron, *The medieval Guildhall of London*, 1974

Nick Bateman, 'The London amphitheatre: excavations 1987–95', *Britannia* 28, 1997

Robert Henri Bautier, *The Economic development of medieval Europe*, 1971

David Bomgardner, *The story of the Roman amphitheatre*, 2000

Lindsey Davis, *Two for the lions*, 1998

Henry Harben, *A dictionary of London*, 1918

Stephen Inwood, *A history of London*, 1998

Gustav Milne, *Roman London*, 1995

R Mitchell & M Leys, *A history of London life*, 1958

Museum of London Archaeology Service, *The archaeology of Greater London*, 2000

H T Riley, *Memorials of London*, 1868

John Schofield, *The building of London from the Conquest to the Great Fire*, 1984

John Stow, *The Survey of London 1598* (ed C L Kingsford 1908)

Thomas Wiedemann, *Emperors and gladiators*, 1992

Glynn Williams, *Medieval London: from commune to capital*, 1963

A mid

11th-century lead-tin brooch

with glass bead inset

The amphitheatre walls boxed up for protection

at the end of the excavations, before the new

Art Gallery was erected over and under it

Index

Nick Bateman led the Museum of London's excavations at Guildhall and is involved in continuing research and publication of the results. He has supervised several important excavations of Roman and medieval London, as well as digs in Italy, and is a Senior Project Manager at the Museum of London Archaeology Service.

The author is grateful to the following institutions and individuals for permission to reproduce illustrations on the pages indicated: courtesy of Terry Ball / English Heritage (69); by permission of the British Library, Stowe 944 fol 6 detail (59); by courtesy of the Trustees of the British Museum (24, 39); by courtesy of the Syndics of Cambridge University Library, Hare A.1 f.276v (60); copyright Colchester Archaeological Trust (39); Judith Dobie (26/27, 29, 52/53); Peter Froste (12); Galleria Borghese, Rome (15); Guildhall Library, Corporation of London (5, 8, 9, 50, 62, 65, 67, 68, 70, 71, 72, 77, 83, 84, 85, 86); copyright Handmade Films (21); Peter Jackson (44); reproduced by courtesy of the Mercers' Company (74); © The National Gallery (79); © The Observer (6); John Pearson (6); Phoenix Art Museum – J-L Gérôme, Pollice verso, oil on canvas, 1872 (37); Royal Library of Belgium, Brussels, ms 13076 77 fol 24v (48); Skyscan Balloon Photography Copyright (38); by courtesy of the Sorrel Estate (33, 42); by courtesy of the family of H E Tidmarsh (9); Trinity College Library, Dublin, ms 177 fol 59v (66); reproduced with kind permission of the Tupper family, Bignor Roman Villa, West Sussex (39); copyright © 2000 by Universal City Studios, Inc. Courtesy of US Publishing Rights. All rights reserved (17); courtesy Warner Brothers (29). All other images are Museum of London Archaeology Service / Museum of London. Paragraphs from *Two for the lions* are by kind permission of Lindsey Davis and Century Books.